GW00391193

God Broke the Mould

Nobody like me, Nobody like You

KATY CHRISTOPHER

God Broke the Mould
Katy Christopher

ISBN 978-1-914615-28-3

A CIP catalogue record for this book is available from the British Library.

Published 2022 Tricorn Books, Aspex

42 The Vulcan Building Gunwharf Quays Portsmouth PO1 3BF

Contents

DEDICATION

I dedicate this, my autobiography, to the three most important people in my life; namely Hugh, my wonderful husband of twenty-eight years, and my parents.

I express my heartfelt gratitude to Hugh, my mother and late father for their ever faithful and unconditional love, support and encouragement.

However, above all, I acknowledge the Lord Jesus Christ, to whom I committed my life when I was a teenager.

I know that it is ultimately by God's grace that I have been protected, and that it is through His Holy Spirit's presence and guidance that my life has been so fulfilled and blessed.

Therefore it is with joy and thanksgiving that I also dedicate my life story to the Lord's praise and glory.

Great is thy faithfulness! Great is thy faithfulness! Morning by morning new mercies I see:

All I have needed Thy hand hath provided, Great is thy faithfulness, Lord, unto me. (Thomas O'Chisholm 1866–1960)

£1 from the sale of every copy of this book will be donated to the Cleft Lip and Palate Association. (CLAPA)

ACKNOWLEDGEMENTS

There are so many people to whom I owe much gratitude for their help as I have written this book.

I have received invaluable assistance in the forms of the cover design, proofreading, provision of factual information, constructive advice and criticism, much moral encouragement and prayer support.

Many people have gone 'the extra mile' to help me, implying that nothing was too much trouble. This was particularly true of retired and current staff at Great Ormond Street Children's Hospital (GOSH) when I was doing research for medically related chapters and aspects of my autobiography.

However, whilst I wish to sincerely thank everybody who has assisted me in any way, in particular I record my great appreciation to the following people.

Initially, and of essential importance, I acknowledge and express my heartfelt gratitude to Hugh, my husband, without whose unfailing patience and support I doubt I would have completed my book.

Judy Anderson – Legacy Development Manager, GOSH Children's Charity
Nicholas Baldwin – Archivist, GOSH
Mr Michael Mars – Consultant Orthodontist, GOSH
Barbara Adsett
Richard Blackshire
Judy Bowers – cover design
Rev. Richard and Elaine Brunton
Stephen Brunton
Sally Charman
Elaine and Victor Goh
Ann James
Dr Peter Johnston
Rev. Peter and Noreen King
Michael and Erica Lynn
Rev. Anthony Martlew – primary proofreader
Jean Massey
Dr Brian, Lynne and Amy McDonogh
Phil and Wendy Shepherd
Linda Waites
Last, but by no means least, all the staff Tricorn Books, especially:
Daniel Bernard – Creative Director
Liz Bourne – Editor
Raphilena Bonito – Illustrator

FOREWORD
by Rev. Anthony Martlew

I am grateful to Katy for asking me to pen these few words by way of an introduction to her life story.

Although Katy is only one of millions who have wrestled to overcome major problems in this life, it is her determination of spirit which has triumphed.

Of one thing I am certain, Katy's Christian faith has been her constant companion from her childhood. Many others in similar circumstances have fallen by the wayside, but Christ has always been her guide.

I have every confidence that the reader will be encouraged in life's goals by Katy's story.

INTRODUCTION

The word of the Lord came to me, saying:
'Before I formed you in the womb I knew you, before you were born
I set you apart...
(Jeremiah Ch.1vv4-5a)

From the dawn of God's creation (Genesis Ch.1) until the end of time, no human being will have ever been an accident or a mistake.

All human life is created by God as part of His perfect plan for His world, starting from conception.

Although I have seriously considered writing my autobiography over many years, I firmly believe that it was the Lord who guided me to proceed through a positive comment from a close friend and sister in the Lord.

I received the encouragement shortly prior to the first national lockdown brought about by the Coronavirus pandemic in March 2020, and felt that lockdown was a confirmation of the Lord leading me to start writing my life story.

A further confirmation that this was the Lord's timing was the realisation that both Hugh and myself were approaching our sixtieth birthdays within the next few months. Therefore, that pending milestone seemed a perfect time to testify to God's presence in my life, what He had enabled me to achieve and how He had used me for His service to date.

There are many verses of Scripture which are very special to me in the course of my Christian walk.

One particularly meaningful text is Jeremiah Ch.29v11, which reads: "'For I know the plans I have for you,' declares the Lord. Plans to prosper and not to harm you, plans to give you a hope and a future.'" Within my book I share principal stages and seasons of my life, including both extremely positive periods and events, but also substantial challenges, because, even through very hard times, I can look back and see, understand and witness how the Lord kept and protected me and used difficult circumstances for my good to bring glory to Him.

The words of the final verse of Graham Kendrick's song,

'Rejoice, Rejoice, Christ is in you' states

"Though we are weak, His grace is everything we need, We're made of clay, but this treasure is within.

He turns our weaknesses into His opportunities, so that the glory goes to Him." (Copyright 1983 Thank You Music.)

Whilst this song must count as an extremely old song now, having been written in the 1980s, it remains extremely relevant to my testimony respecting challenges which I have encountered in life.

The prophet Zephaniah states:

"The Lord your God is with you, the mighty warrior who saves. He will take great delight in you; in his love He will no longer rebuke you, but will rejoice over you with singing." (Ch.3v17)

Whilst some of my autobiography is quite serious, I hope that, overall, my story will prove fairly easy reading and raise some smiles and chuckles in places.

However, most importantly of all, I hope that it will be a real encouragement that the Lord loves us all with an everlasting love and has drawn us with unfailing kindness (Jeremiah Ch.31vv3-4)

If we allow him to, the Lord can and will work powerfully and greatly bless us by His Holy Spirit.

CHAPTER ONE
EARLY YEARS

'For I know the plans I have for you', declares the Lord, 'plans to prosper you and not to harm you; plans to give you a hope and a future.'
(Jeremiah Ch.29v11)

Whilst I have been known by my preferred name; Katy for many years now, my legal names are Katherine Janet. (When in my thirties I added Louise as an extra family name.)

I was born on 10 June 1960 in St Paul's Hospital, Hemel Hempstead, in Hertfordshire. My family home was in Abbots langley between Hemel Hempstead and Watford

My parents were Frank Massey and Beatrice Mary Semper.

I was a big baby, weighing in at a few ounces over nine pounds. However, this was partially due to the fact that I was about three weeks overdue, which would not have occurred nowadays.

On learning my name and birth weight , a quick-witted relative dubbed me 'Katherine the Great'! In colouring and features, I definitely took after my father. I had a mass of dark-brown curly hair with a round face. When I was a year old, a photograph was taken of me, which was strikingly similar to one of my father at the same age, and many people commented on my resemblance to him.

My mother stayed in hospital for about a fortnight following my birth, which was quite usual in the early 1960s – especially with a first baby. Shortly after birth I was routinely examined by a doctor, and my mother noticed him looking closely inside my mouth, which seemed odd to her, but the doctor made no comments at the time.

However, the next day my parents were told that I had been born with a cleft palate, which is a congenital defect where the roof of the mouth does not fuse together properly. Fortunately, I was not affected by a cleft lip. Thus in due course, my parents could take pride and delight in showing me off to doting family, friends and neighbours.

Because antenatal scans did not exist in the early 1960s, birth conditions and defects were quite an issue, because there were no warnings that a baby had a deformity whilst growing in the womb.

Nevertheless, all parents naturally want their children to be born perfectly healthy, and it was inevitably a shock to my parents to learn that I had a condition which would require hospital treatment including surgery throughout my childhood.

In 1960 the nearest hospital to Abbots Langley which treated clefts was the world-famous Hospital for Sick Children, Great Ormond Street, London. In recent years the hospital was renamed 'Great Ormond Street Hospital for Children', popularly referred to as 'GOSH'. From now on I shall refer to it as such.

Having been referred to GOSH by St Paul's Hospital, my first appointment there took place in autumn 1960 when I was about four months old.

That initial appointment at GOSH duly proved to be my first experience of the lifelong association which I would form with the hospital.

GOSH became an extremely important part of my life, through both my hospital treatment and as part of my Christian testimony, as I share in relevant parts of my book, especially chapter four.

Whilst not a life-threatening condition in the Western world, a cleft palate significantly affects feeding, speech, dentition and often appearance as affected people reach adolescence. Hearing can also be affected, although happily I was not affected by that issue.

I was taken home from St Paul's Hospital when I was about two weeks old. With advances in medical science and invention of aids, in current generations special items of equipment can be provided to help with feeding for babies born with clefts, but in my infancy, such items were not available.

Breastfeeding and the use of baby bottles with teats were not viable options because the cleft prevented me from sucking. Thus, feeding me was an intricate and very time-consuming procedure, ultimately achieved by my parents feeding me miniscule amounts at a time with a teaspoon.

Although my parents understood that this would take longer than standard feeding, after some days, their worries increased, as I did not seem to show any interest in food, which made an already very difficult job even more stressful. My parents began to wonder if I had another underlying issue, because, in addition to the feeding problems, I seemed unable to stay awake during their efforts to feed me. In fact, I only seemed to want to sleep, discounting the fact that I was a newborn baby.

My immediate family was very small and I had no direct cousins or contemporaries with whom my parents could compare me to feel sure that they were not worrying unnecessarily.

My mother contacted the health visitor, who visited me and endorsed my parents' concerns that I was not as alert as I should have been, even considering the fact that I was still only three weeks old.

We had an excellent GP in the late Dr Peter Tomson, whom the health visitor consulted, and very soon afterwards I was taken to see him. On examination, the GP suspected a hormone condition and contacted a colleague who was a relevant (endocrine) specialist at GOSH and lived comparatively near us in Hertfordshire.

The specialist agreed to visit me at our home, together with our GP, and I was diagnosed as suffering from Congenital Hypothyroidism (CH), which meant that I had been born without a thyroid gland.

A blood test confirmed the diagnosis when I was still only six weeks old. Therefore, the span of time between my parents expressing their concerns to the health visitor, the home visit and diagnosis was miraculously quick. God really blessed me in having parents who were sufficiently astute to raise their concerns so promptly, and an attentive health visitor, GP and consultant who were so willing to go the extra mile and do all they did. The specialist explained to my parents that I would need to take the medication Levothyroxine for life, in order to replace the hormone which I was not receiving through not having my thyroid gland.

My parents had to crush the tablets and mix them with my milk, and, progressively, my food, until I reached the age at which I was able to swallow them myself with a drink.

With my CH diagnosis and commencement of my taking my medication, a major battle was won.

Within days of starting to take the tablets, I became extremely wakeful, alert and interested in taking in all the milk that my parents were trying to feed me – as quickly as possible. Although the feeding process was still slow, seeing me thriving made their efforts well worthwhile!

I think that those initial weeks of my life were the only ones when there were ever any significant concerns respecting my reluctance to feed and whether I was gaining sufficient weight!

I had my first cleft-palate repair operation at fifteen months old, which was the average age for such surgery, especially as I did not have a cleft lip. I was in hospital for two weeks, which must have been extremely difficult for my parents, since the philosophy respecting children's hospital admission was completely different to nowadays, with strong parental involvement and positive relationships between parents and medical professionals being the norm. In current generations, parents can virtually always stay in hospital with children, so are with them during treatment.

When surgery is involved, parents can be present when children go to sleep and wake up, so in their minds, their parents never left them.

By stark contrast, when I had my first surgery in 1961, visiting was at set times, with no visiting at all being allowed on operation days. Whilst GOSH is exclusively a children's hospital and children were treated compassionately by the nurses, specialists' and doctors' focuses were more upon the children's treatment rather than child-friendly and parental- professional attitudes. My parents must have been exhausted, both emotionally and practically, as they travelled to visit me almost every day. My first operation proceeded as successfully as hoped and expected.

Following this surgery and post-operative check-up, I visited GOSH for annual reviews, but did not require further surgery until 1968.

My parents found GOSH quite thought-provoking when they took me there for appointments in my infancy and earliest childhood. I think that they were very shocked by some children that they saw, who were obviously extremely disabled.

My parents told me that they felt like frauds when they saw such children, then looked at me who showed no signs as to why I was at GOSH since I looked completely 'normal' and healthy.

However, due to my cleft, my first tooth did not come through until I was about eighteen months, and whilst I had my initial repair surgery at fifteen months old, my speech was not at all intelligible until I was about three.

I could say words and make sounds which immediate family could understand, and I am certain that I would have made my needs, wants and feelings perfectly clear! However, clarity was always a problem which set me apart from my peers as I grew up and led to inevitable frustration when I was not easily understood by people other than those who knew me really well, such as close family.

Whilst I could not help my voice and speech with respect to physiological issues, I didn't help myself in that, when I was eventually able to talk with some measure of clarity, I proved myself to be a real chatterbox! (Family, friends and all who know me well would probably say that situation has not noticeably changed, although my clarity and quality of speech is much better – as long as I remember to speak slowly.)

I was said to take after my maternal grandfather and a few aunts, all of whom could talk the hind leg off a donkey! Nevertheless, whilst they would laugh if people referred to the issue, due to my impediment, I was very sensitive to any reference to my speech until recent years.

Because of my CH, throughout infancy, childhood and adolescence, I had annual blood tests and review appointments at our GP surgery and local hospital, to ensure that I was taking the correct dosage of my medication, especially as I grew. However, since adulthood CH-related issues have normally been successfully monitored by my GP.

I was extremely blessed that my immediate family loved me and supported me fully with regards to my medical problems, which must have caused much concern, especially for my parents.

My parents married comparatively later than average, and were both in their thirties when I was born, Due to a combination of my parents being older first-time parents and my being born with medical conditions which required ongoing treatment and medication, I proved to be their only child.

My parents did not completely rule out the possibility of having a second child, and sought the opinions of medical professionals about the risk of a second child being born with the same conditions as myself, especially the cleft. However, whilst told by doctors that the chance of a repeat was almost zero, my parents met other families at GOSH who had been given the same assurance, only for a second child to be born with a cleft. Thus, my parents ultimately made the decision to concentrate on enjoying me and giving me the best upbringing that they could. I never lacked for anything, and, most importantly of all, knew my parents' unconditional love and acceptance.

However, my medical conditions and related issues did not render me stupid, and certainly did not make me immune from wrongdoing! I strongly refute the concept that only children are spoilt brats who can never do wrong in their parents' eyes! I was perfectly capable of trying my parents' patience to the uttermost, whether or not intentionally! As recorded in chapter two, my parents met at music college, my mother being a pianist and my father a singer. However following their marriage in 1957 and my birth three years later, whilst my mother made her entire career in music, my father kept music as a serious hobby and pursued secure employment with regular hours in order to reliably provide for my mother and myself.

My mother taught in schools and built up a private piano-teaching practice at home, whilst my father worked as a clerical/administrative officer for both the NHS and local government. Additionally, my father worked alternate weekends as a switchboard operator at Watford Hospital, for some years in order to earn extra income.

My mother left school teaching shortly before my birth until 1969, but continued her private piano-teaching practice which she was able to combine with looking after our home and myself, faithfully supported by my father. My parents took their roles extremely seriously, sharing all aspects of my care and upbringing.

During infancy and pre-school years, my mother did housework and cared for me until mid-afternoons when she taught junior school pupils until father came home from work. After the evening meal, my father cleared up and took over my care including bathing me and putting me to bed whilst my mother taught senior school pupils in the early evenings. Therefore, my parents had their time together once my mother had finished teaching.

During my first year of life, my mother could teach her afternoon pupils whilst I was asleep in my carry cot, which fitted very neatly underneath our grand piano!

However, as I became a toddler and beyond, mothers of junior school age pupils would look after me in our dining room, whilst my mother taught their children.

My maternal grandparents lived in South Ruislip, Middlesex, which was comparatively near, and my grandad drove, so they visited most weeks, and could look after me, including picking me up from school once relevant.

My parents did all they possibly could to give me a happy home and childhood, and tried to ensure that I had as much contact as possible with other children, being an only child. With my father also having been an only child, and my mother's sister and husband having no children, I had no direct cousins. However both of my parents had direct cousins, whose families were my contemporaries. Thus, I had an extended family, all of whom accepted and treated me as a direct niece and cousin. As years progressed, I forged very close relationships with some of these relatives and their families, to the point where we consider each other as honorary brothers and sisters, nieces, nephews and beyond! In addition, I grew up with families of my parents' friends, and my mother took me to crèches and parents and children's groups prior to starting school, since pre-school education in my generation was not standard as it has been more recently.

Overall, however, from birth until I started school in 1965, my family – both immediate and extended – were my bedrock which, praise God, was a trustworthy bedrock of love and entire security.

When considering my immediate family and my character/personality, I feel that I inherited my serious side from my parents and extrovert and sense of fun and humour from grandparents, especially from what I was told about my paternal grandmother and knew from my paternal grandfather – to the cost of family, friends and all who have known me well during my life!

Although no human beings are perfect, a close friend told me that God had chosen me as the perfect child for my parents and vice versa. I think that statement was true respecting all of my immediate family, without whom I would not have experienced the childhood and life which I have had. There but for the grace of God go I.

CHAPTER TWO
MUSIC TO THE EARS

Sing and make music from your heart to the Lord, always giving thanks to
God the Father for everything in the name of our Lord Jesus
Christ. (Ephesians Ch.5vv19b-20)

According to the theory that babies hear sounds and sense atmospheres
whilst growing in the womb, I definitely registered a musical influence
prior to my birth!

Both of my parents were very musical and from early childhood, I
showed that I had inherited their musical gifts. My father was a singer and
my mother was a pianist.

In childhood, my father possessed a fine treble voice, then proceeded to
demonstrate his strong musical interest during senior school years.

During the war, my father was a member of the Fleet Air Arm in Scotland,
during which time he participated in many musical shows. Following
demobilisation, he continued singing prior to commencing a full-time
professional course at the London College of Music (LCM).

My mother learnt the piano from eight years old, and demonstrated
exceptional talent throughout childhood and adolescence, despite evacuation
during the war totally halting tuition for about four years. After school she did
clerical work in London, whilst studying the piano privately with Geoffrey
Sayers, who was also a highly regarded piano teacher at the LCM. With Mr
Sayers' encouragement, my mother entered for and won a scholarship to
study full time at the LCM and continue studying with him there.

My parents met soon after my mother started at LCM, and she duly
became my father's regular accompanist, as well as being a concert pianist
in various vicinities of London in addition to her studies.

Both of my parents graduated with their LLCM diplomas. (Licentiate of
the London College of Music) In addition, my mother achieved prestigious
diplomas in both piano teaching and performance, the latter of which was
always her proudest achievement.

Following graduation, my father spent some happy years touring the
United Kingdom as a singer and entertainer in the *Black and White Minstrel
Show*, ice shows, pantomimes, summer season entertainment and being on
television in the days of its infancy.

At what could probably be described as being at completely the other end of the performance spectrum, my father also loved choral singing and was frequently an oratorio soloist, his favourite oratorio always being 'Elijah' by Mendelssohn.

My mother gained her school-teaching qualification, after which her career combined school and a private piano-teaching practice.

Whilst my parents' paths differed for those few years, they eventually met up again and formed a deep relationship, which led to a very happy marriage of nearly forty-eight years until my father passed away in 2005. My parents gained great pleasure from playing and singing together, attending concerts and listening to music together on the radio, television and records. Whilst my parents appreciated most genres of classical music, one of my mother's definite passions was Wagnerian opera.

Throughout married life, music occupied much of my mother's life; being both her career and greatest pleasure. However, as previously shared, my father sought secure employment with regular hours whilst reserving music as his serious hobby.

Once born, I was surrounded by music, and photographs taken of me during my infancy and early childhood included a fair number with me seated at the piano.

My mother began to teach me to play the piano when I was four until 1967, when I commenced tuition at the Watford School of Music (WSM) where I also attended theory/musicianship and singing classes during junior school years.

I was accepted as a piano student of Jean Merlow, which was an enormous privilege, because she taught exceptionally talented students who won prestigious competitions and duly gained critical acclaim for themselves in the world of music.

I achieved my grades one to five exams with Miss Merlow, chiefly gaining merit category marks, although I achieved the distinction category in grade five; distinction being Jean Merlow's true definition of success. In 1974 my parents felt that I would benefit from a change of teacher at the WSM, so after consultation with the principal I was offered tuition with David Martin, whom I studied with from 1974–1978.

In wishing me well, Miss Merlow told me that I would be capable of achieving my grade eight exam in due course, which was a tremendous accolade and encouragement from her.

I gained fresh encouragement and ideas from Mr Martin, and from 1975–1977 I received very creditable results in my grades six to eight exams including merit in grade seven, and my tuition with Mr Martin ended very positively in 1978 when I gained distinction in grade five general musicianship.

From comparatively soon after beginning to learn the piano until I left school, I participated in concerts and music festivals. With respect to the latter, I frequently received very positive assessments from adjudicators, both in solo classes and duet classes, which I entered with a friend who was a pupil of my mother.

As well as music studies at the WSM, I was also strongly involved in music at junior and senior school. Both my parents and myself were always extremely anxious for me to be able to attend Longdean School, Hemel Hempstead for my secondary education, due to the very high reputation of its music department.

In due course I was allocated a place at Longdean, in my lower school years of which the Head of Music was Christopher Pearson, and the music staff included Margaret Jefferies (née Killick), both of whom were held in extremely high regard in the local area.

Due to Longdean's strong musical tradition and reputation, the first-year music syllabus was strongly academic, including reading music, music theory and in-depth study of classical compositions. The syllabus incorporated weekly homework assignments, tests and a summer exam.

In the second and third years, pupils who were musically gifted and interested in classical/choral music could join a specialist music class taught by Mr Pearson, including both theoretical and practical music. In the third year, pupils had the option of sitting the grade five theory exam which would be required for entering the top practical grade exams and about half of the class chose music as an O-level option.

Longdean's choir and orchestra had an excellent reputation locally, the former formed of pupils from the first year to sixth-formers and a fair number of staff.

The choir and orchestra performed varied concerts, and major choral works such as Handel's *Messiah*, Vivaldi's *Gloria* and J. S. Bach's *Magnificat* and *St John Passion*. Performances took place at school, in various churches and concert venues in Hemel Hempstead and Chesham when we combined with the Chesham Singers for the performances of the *St John Passion*.

When Mr Pearson left at the end of my third year at Longdean, he was succeeded by Julian Larkin, who was an equally competent and pleasant teacher. Commencing O-level and CSE courses as Mr Larkin arrived, I was one of the first class of O-level courses which he taught at Longdean as Head of Music.

Having formerly been the assistant organist of Portsmouth Cathedral, Mr Larkin, strongly promoted church music within the choir's repertoire. When Mr Larkin realised that I was in my church choir and was seriously interested in church music, he asked me if I would be interested in learning the organ with him. Whilst my instinctive reaction was enormous enthusiasm, after serious discussion with my parents, I very reluctantly made my own decision that scheduling organ practice at church on top of schoolwork, piano and violin practice would prove too much to cope with in that period in my life. (When I ultimately began organ tuition some years later, I frequently felt that I should have taken up the organ with Mr Larkin when at school in place of the violin!)

The Longdean music department was a very positive area with which to be involved. With classical and choral music being specialist/minority interests, a sense of comradeship existed between like-minded staff and students across the school. I definitely fulfilled the chief purpose for attending Longdean for most of my senior education; namely all the musical opportunities and activities which I immensely enjoyed.

My move to Watford Grammar School for Girls (WGGS) for the sixth-form occurred at an opportune time, because the choirs and orchestras of the girls' and boys' grammar schools had just begun to combine to perform significant choral works, such as Haydn's *Creation* and Rossini's *Stabat Mater*.

Being an A-level music student, membership of the WGGS senior choir was compulsory, although I would definitely have joined even if not obliged to do so.

Both Watford grammar schools had a strong Christian ethos, and the WGGS senior choir played a prominent role in assemblies, the three traditional services of Nine Lessons and Carols and the annual Founder's Day service which was held in the main Watford Parish church.

Because the A-level music course included practical prerequisites and requirements, A-level music students received free instrumental tuition for the duration of the course – much to the delight of my parents (and myself when they decided to allocate the tuition fees to me as a clothing allowance!)

Having passed my O-level music, I felt very pleased to be able to study for my A-level music, although I was not certain if I had the ability to do so. Teachers at both my junior school and Longdean had always predicted that I should be able to obtain reasonable O-level/CSE results, but had never promised me that I would be able to achieve A-levels. Therefore, both my parents and myself were delighted when I learned that I had passed my A-level music with grade D – a grade to spare.

Between autumn 1978 and the end of 1980 I underwent major oral surgery and related treatments, so applying for higher education or employment was not feasible during that period (see chapter seven).

In early 1980, my parents paid for me to begin organ tuition whilst I had plenty of time to attend lessons and practice. I gained much satisfaction from my tuition, my original inspiration to learn the organ stemmed from seeing and hearing the GOSH chapel organ when an inpatient in 1968 (see chapter four).

I learned the organ in churches in Watford between 1980 and 1986. I had two teachers during those years, both of whom were excellent and held the highest attainable organ diploma. I was also greatly blessed to be allowed unlimited free practice on the organ in my own church in those years.

I achieved my grade four organ exam with a hight merit in autumn 1980, then between 1981and 1984 I achieved my grades six, seven and eight exams and grade eight theory, all with merit except for grade seven in which I narrowly missed the merit category.

In early 1982 I gained my first employment in the Civil Service in Watford, whilst continuing my organ studies and, together with my mother, teaching piano privately at home in my own time.

Due to the enormous satisfaction that I gained from playing the organ and teaching, I began to seriously consider applying for a course of study leading to a professional musical qualification, and in 1985 I made a definite decision to do so.

John Winter, one of my organ tutors, told me that Colchester Institute had a music school which ran highly regarded courses, so I duly obtained a prospectus.

Colchester Institute School of Music (CISM) offered two undergraduate courses which led to either a BA (Hons) degree or Graduate Diploma in Music (GD). Being twenty-five, I was eligible to apply for a degree course as a mature student, which meant that CISM staff would consider my application, although I did not possess all the educational qualifications which were normally required to be accepted for degree courses. On studying the prospectus, I was very inspired to learn that one major option for the BA course was Christian Liturgical Music, and on completion of reading the prospectus I filled in the application form. However, with my characteristic impetuousness, I misread the question on the form, respecting the course for which I was applying. Therefore, instead of writing 'BA (Hons)' or 'GD' I wrote 'Christian Liturgical Music (CLM)', which was the major option which I would choose to take in my second/third years! I submitted my application form, and in due course was invited for an audition at the CISM.

On the day of my audition, I discovered that William Tamblyn, the principal of the CISM, was also the tutor for the CLM option, so I realised in retrospect that my error on my application form probably worked in my favour when the principal initially read it!

I was impressed with the tutor who conducted my audition and interview, and felt that the occasion proceeded quite well and I did myself justice. I apparently did, since, comparatively soon after my audition, I heard that I had been accepted on the BA course commencing in September 1986. I was also informed that I would receive a mandatory grant because the course led to an honours degree.

My parents and I were obviously delighted, and the course duly proved to be a classic example of my ability to achieve anything that I set my heart on, even if my goal was possibly beyond my natural ability. I was certain that if I passed my first year (identical for BA and GD students), I would achieve my degree, because the second/third years would include major options and supporting components.

My parents and I visited Colchester prior to the start of my course, in order to meet the family in whose home I would live during my first year, in addition to visiting the CISM and town.

The course commenced in mid-September with Freshers' week, which typically involved enrolment, auditions respecting allocation to tutors for course components and practical studies (mine being organ and piano), varied introductory meetings and social events.

I was always very happy with all my course tutors, academic, instrumental and personal, and overall my three years at CISM were extremely positive from the perspectives of the course itself, the social aspects and (especially) my faith which deepened considerably in those years (see chapter twelve). One course component was 'Related Studies', for which students had to submit assignments on arts subjects which were not primarily connected with music. This was because the degree courses available at CISM (especially the BA course) were 'arts' courses with music being the primary subject, rather than exclusively music degrees (such as BMus).

During my first term at CISM, I was anxious about the assessments of my first essays, because I was unsure of the required standard for success in degree assignments. Therefore I was both relived and happy when my results proved to exceed the required grades.

Whilst the CISM hosted several choirs and orchestras, the chief choir and orchestra were degree-course components, so it was compulsory for

BA/GD students to be a member of one or the other. Neither of my practical studies being orchestral instruments I was obviously in the choir, with which I was perfectly happy having always loved singing.

The chief works performed by the choir and orchestra in my first year were Elgar's *The Music Makers* and Benjamin Britten's *War Requiem*, which we performed at Snape Maltings, in Aldeburgh, Suffolk.

During my first year, I was also a member of the chamber choir, with my favourite work being the cantata 'St Nicholas' by Benjamin Britten.

At the end of my first year at CISM I was very happy to learn that I had passed my first year with the required prerequisite grades to proceed to my second year and take up my first-choice major option of CLM, in addition to second-year core components Music History/Literature, Related Studies and continuation of practical studies.

The criteria for the CLM option comprised four elements:

History of Church Music: From the earliest centuries up to the present generation.

Liturgical Composition: Students were required to submit a portfolio of compositions of varied styles and traditions of Christian music which might be played within the context of corporate worship.

Church Placement: Students took active involvement in the worship of a particular church under the supervision of the Director of Music/Worship for the two-year duration of the CLM option. Students were required to submit a comprehensive placement project respecting their church, which documented all their involvement with regards the music and worship. Students' supervisors were required to submit reports twice per year and the CLM tutor would visit students' churches periodically to assess their participation and involvement.

Whilst virtually all students undertook placements at churches within the vicinity of Colchester, the CLM tutor supported my request to travel home most weekends in order to undertake my placement at St Nicholas, Elstree, where I was the official organist/Director of Music, whilst released for college commitments in term time. The rector strongly supported me respecting placement requirements, and submitting required reports to the CLM tutor, who willingly travelled up to Elstree twice to conduct his own assessment of my involvement.

1988 marked the octocentenary of St Nicholas, Elstree, so special services and events took place throughout the year. Therefore, the recording of such occasions offered a unique element to my CLM placement project, in addition to standard required records and information.

Extended Essay: Students were required to submit an extended essay on a relevant aspect of Christian music which was approved by the CLM tutor.

My subject was cathedral choirs with and without choir schools. My primary case studies were Liverpool Metropolitan, St Edmundsbury, Wells and Westminster cathedrals. However, in addition I also contacted and visited other cathedrals, and overall received much assistance from cathedral music staff and choristers, including being invited to spend an incredible amount of time at each of the cathedrals on which I primarily focused. My visits took place during my second year, as did my research visit to York Minster, having chosen to write my Related Studies extended essay on the restoration of the Minster's South Transept, following the fire which occurred in 1984.

My research for my Related Studies and CLM extended essays respectively proved perfect opportunities to put long-term serious interests to constructive academic use!

Periodically, the Head of CLM took CLM students on a day visiting churches in Essex and Suffolk, which were relevant to our option, from architectural and/or musical perspectives. Due to visiting about five to six churches in a day, the trips were humorously dubbed 'church crawls'! Whilst part of our course, the days usually included pub lunches, so always proved to be true combinations of study and pleasure!

There was a healthy diversity of denominations amongst CLM students, ranging from Anglo/Roman Catholicism to Elim Pentecostalism, and in my third year two Greek Orthodox students joined the mix! We related to each other really well, sharing our own worship traditions and respecting those of each other. During my final term, we all attended services at the Greek Orthodox and Elim Pentecostal churches, both occasions being revelations for students unused to the respective forms of worship!

Having successfully completed my second-year assignments, including a 2:1 for my extended essay on York Minster, I progressed to an extremely busy final year at CISM.

The final year core syllabus included Music History/Literature, for which two written assignments were required (including an extended essay), submission of written assignments respecting our major options and our final year first and second practical study recitals – organ students performing their recitals on fine instruments housed in churches in Colchester.

In addition to studies, all students were involved in rehearsing Elgar's *Dream of Gerontius,* for which we combined with the University of Essex, performing at the university and Snape Maltings respectively. I felt that those performances were a fitting conclusion to a very happy three years of my life, and I duly added *The Dream of Gerontius* to my list of favourite oratorios!

On top of preparation for final assessments for my degree and choir performances, during my final year at CISM, I sat the Archbishops' Certificate in Church Music exam. The syllabus of the certificate (A CertCM) covered much of the CLM option, thus enabling me to use a significant amount of my CLM work towards the two essays which were required, and revision for the written examinations.

I entered for the exam on the strong encouragement of the CLM tutor, who was involved with the revision of the Roman Catholic syllabus for the exam, the certificate being a qualification jointly awarded by the Archbishops of Canterbury and Westminster.

Entering the exam as a chorister, the two practical components were achieving grade 5+ in singing and an exam set by the Guild of Church Musicians (GCM) which was the examining body for the certificate. I self-financed six months of singing lessons with a CISM singing teacher to work for the practical exams, both of which I passed in spring 1989. I took the grade five exam in Colchester, and the GCM exam in Elstree church, for which my mother accompanied me on the organ for the hymn, psalm and anthem, which were the musical requirements of the exam.

Parts three and four of the certificate concerned Christian Worship and The History and General Knowledge of Church Music. Certificate candidates were allowed three years in which to successfully complete all parts of the syllabus in order to achieve the qualification.

Obviously the combination of achieving requirements for the final year of my degree, the ACertCM and concert rehearsals did not allow much leisure time in the academic year of 1988–1989!

The submission deadline for all final year BA/GD written projects and assignments was mid-May, with practical study final recitals, viva voces and CISM competitions taking place during June.

On submission of my degree work, I turned my attention to the writing and submission of my two essays for the ACertCM, the subject titles concerning Scripture in Worship and S.S. Wesley. However, with the A Cert.CM exams being in July, I was able to postpone revision until I left the CISM.

When the BA/GD degree results were issued and displayed in the CISM, I felt amazed to see my name amongst the students who had achieved a 2:2 honours degree, having been originally accepted on the course with fewer educational qualifications than normally required for entry to degree courses.

My BA completed, I returned home and prepared for my ACertCM written exams, which I sat in the Elstree rectory, with the rector serving as my invigilator, after which I could finally relax during the summer!

About six weeks later I received a letter from the GCM registrar informing me that I had passed both written components of the ACertCM exam. Therefore, having previously passed the practical exams, I had gained the qualification. The letter proceeded to give information about the presentation of the certificate in November, and also included a request for my consent to publish my Christian Worship essay in a future issue of the GCM magazine due to the high mark which it was awarded.

Having sat the ACertCM exam concurrently with completing my degree, on learning that I had gained the entire Archbishops' certificate in one year, whilst happy once the news sunk in, my instinctive reaction was one of genuine amazement to the point of shock! With all that I had been involved in that academic year, I genuinely thought that if I had passed one written component of the certificate exam I would have done really well, then could resit the other component and gain my award the next year. In contrast, my parents – especially my father – would not admit to being surprised, they were just delighted!

The presentation of certificates took place during Evensong in the chapel of Lambeth Palace chapel on All Saints' Day 1989, followed by my BA degree ceremony at the CISM three days later. Whilst I had realised that both events occurred within the same week, it had never occurred to me that I would be attending both ceremonies in the same year.

Following the presentation of the ACertCM, all recipients and two guests were invited to the palace drawing room for afternoon tea, my guests obviously being my parents. The Archbishop of Canterbury at that time was Robert Runcie, which was special for my parents and myself, since he was formerly Bishop of St Albans, our home diocese.

As with the presentation at Lambeth, the graduation ceremony at CISM was obviously also very special, taking place in the CISM concert hall. After the presentation of degrees and awards, a short piano recital was given by the famous concert pianist, John Lill, of whom my mother was a great admirer.

Following graduation, I resumed living with my parents in Abbots Langley due to financial reasons and, as prior to college days, I combined employment in the Civil Service with organ playing and private tuition at home, flexible working hours enabling me to play for midweek services, such as funerals, as required.

When Hugh and I set up home in Lancing following our wedding, I built up my own freelance music career, consisting of playing the organ and private teaching prior to the Lord leading me down a new path through my organ work after some years.

Whilst chapters eight/nine of this book focus on my career, because this chapter focuses upon the musical impact in my life, it is relevant to state that after many years of music taking second place in my working life, I was ultimately able to make it music my primary career.

When Hugh and I met, we quickly discovered our mutual interest in the organ, both as an instrument for worship (as recorded in relevant parts of this book) and a musical instrument in its own right, with playing different organs and attending organ recitals being a serious interest.

Living locally to Lancing College, we are fortunate to be able to attend excellent organ recitals in the college chapel. The chapel houses two fine organs which attract many distinguished recitalists. One organ is a two-manual organ at the east end of the chapel, which was built by the Dutch firm Frobenius, and the other instrument is a four-manual Walker organ, which sits on the West gallery.

I have been privileged to have had opportunities to play the organs of many cathedrals and collegiate chapel organs. I have always been amazed by the welcoming attitudes of organists and directors of music when I have contacted them to request permission to view organs at close quarters and play them. Favourite experiences have included Coventry, Ely and St Albans Cathedrals, York Minster, St George's Chapel, Windsor, Lancing College, New College and Christchurch Cathedral, Oxford.

Favourite music genres of Hugh and myself include choral and organ music, Baroque, Classic and Romantic orchestral and piano music. For my mother's sake, I regret never cultivating a passion for opera!

Originally I did not wish to follow a musical career because music incorporates so many facets from both professional and amateur perspectives. Therefore I was afraid that the two might overlap, with the result that I became 'swamped' by music and consequently lost my interest in and love of it entirely. However, in retrospect, I came to realise the complete opposite was true, and I appreciated the gift of music in all spheres of life, whether through personal participation or the joy of listening to live or recorded music. Whilst close family and friends knew how I felt, many people who knew me wondered how I could have considered any career other than music.

I admit that I have sometimes wondered what path my life might have taken, had I aspired to a musical career from childhood or adolescence, since my long-term ambition was nursing, so I achieved grade eight in three subjects and A-level music simply for 'pleasure'!

However, as affirmed throughout the course of my autobiography, it was clearly the Lord who directed my path; not least because my life was so complex to understand at times!

Nevertheless, whether from the perspective of performing or listening to music, I greatly appreciate the substantially integral part which music has 'played' in and had upon my life.

CHAPTER THREE
PRIMARY AGE THRILLS AND SPILLS

I can do all things through Christ who gives me strength.
(Philippians Ch.4v13)

In the early 1960s there was a significant baby boom, the consequence of which was that children could not normally start school until the September in which they were five years of age. Thus, children such as myself, whose birthdays fell in the final quarter of the English academic year, only spent two years in infant school, effectively missing a year's education.

However, as a teacher, my mother realised that I would be at an educational disadvantage, so my parents taught me to read, alongside elementary number work, so that I would be on a par with my contemporaries when I started school in 1965.

My learning ability was not at all affected by either my cleft palate or my lack of thyroid gland (CH) since I was diagnosed and thus began medication so miraculously early. Therefore my parents took pride in the fact that whilst I was obviously not 'Brain of Britain', I achieved all my educational milestones and overall was always classed as a 'good average' at school.

Whilst both my parents took a serious and active interest in my education, my father was a particular driving force in that sphere, always encouraging me to exceed standard requirements for my peer group. In addition to overseeing and helping me with schoolwork, my father taught me to spell many words which were considerably beyond the average vocabulary for my school year, and times tables for numbers beyond the level that my class had reached.

My father's philosophy was that although I had definite medical conditions, if I always worked to the best of my ability and achieved positive results in my music studies and education generally, I would be recognised for my achievements as much as, or even more than, my medical issues. Whilst my father could sound hard to please, he always stated that he felt that I would achieve anything I wanted, and in the majority of cases in my life I believe that I proved him right.

I always valued the positive mindset that both my parents instilled within me, and consequently I have always put my best effort into everything that I have undertaken in life. Throughout all stages of my schooling, whether at parents' evenings or written in reports, teachers nearly always stated that I always worked to the best of my ability.

When I was six I joined Explorers, the first section of the Girls' Brigade at Abbots Langley Baptist Church, where I attended junior church throughout my childhood.

Once I started at junior school, I joined lunchtime clubs, and my age group at Girls' Brigade moved up to the junior section, all these activities being in addition to piano lessons and musical activities at the Watford School of Music. Enjoying all the activities in which I was involved, being grounded served as a primary threat or reality of discipline meted out for misdemeanours!

In due course, pets took up residence in our home. These were chiefly budgerigars, which we bred for a number of years and housed in a small aviary in addition to our 'pet' budgie indoors. However, shortly before Christmas 1970, we acquired a gorgeous eight-month-old Manchester terrier/border collie from a rescue centre. Whilst Shandy ('Shan') was my chief Christmas present from my parents that year, obviously we all doted on her and she ruled our lives with a rod of iron for thirteen years! Whilst my parents trained Shan to be wonderfully behaved when with us, having been ill-treated as a puppy she could not easily be left. Therefore, Shan went virtually everywhere with us, including on holiday. We had Shan to thank for some wonderful holidays in Ventnor, Isle of Wight, having found a lovely small hotel in a Pets Welcome brochure!

As applicable to all caring parents, much of my parents' lives centred around me: ferrying me to and from music studies/activities, all other activities and social occasions, helping me with/supervising my schoolwork and music practice, and overall doing all they could in order to give me a stable upbringing. In addition to occasions such as birthdays, Christmas time and holidays, I recall many 'normal' pleasures, such as shopping, surprise outings and treats, etc. Overall, I was blessed with a very secure home life, complete with family and friends who knew, accepted and loved me for who I was.

Obviously my parents' responsibilities also included taking me to many medical appointments, obtaining and supervising medication and encouraging my speech practice when I was attending speech therapy. My parents must have found my care overwhelming at times, but, to me, always seemed positive and supportive. Needless to say, we had our arguments, since, apart from reprimands for normal childish misbehaviour, my parents expressed constructive criticism when they felt that I was not helping myself in respect of my health and personal issues, and there were times when I did not appreciate it!

Due to a combination of frustration with myself if I could not easily manage issues and tasks and, admittedly, possessing a strong-willed personality, I was not gifted in listening without answering back or arguing, which frequently resulted in my ending up in more trouble than my wrongdoing or problem in the first place!

Unfortunately, whilst my first palatal repair operation was deemed successful by my consultant, I still had a residual cleft, which was not repaired until I was nearly eight years of age. Thus, during my earliest school years my speech impediment caused problems with communication with my peers until I had my second operation during my first year of junior school. I also experienced significant regurgitation of food and drink, and, because I could not suck, my attempts to drink the school milk with a straw met with total failure, ridicule from contemporaries and scolding from my teacher for using multiple straws, because she, like most other people including my parents, did not realise that with a cleft, using a straw was a totally impossible feat for me. I also displayed much emotional instability, and inevitably all these factors made me a prime target for bullying.

When medical professionals told my parents that I had a cleft palate and CH, they were told the basic facts respecting treatment, such as the facts that I would need surgery to repair my palate and lifelong medication due to my CH. However, my parents were given no information at all regarding potential problems related to my conditions. Classic examples of such issues were the facts that I would not be able to suck until my cleft palate was completely repaired, and CH could cause issues such as emotional anxiety/depression. Not being medical professionals, my parents simply accepted the information that they were told, with the implications that such treatment would 'sort my issues'.

In the 1960s, when in my first years of life, there was a general lack of rapport between medical professionals and parents/children, with the amount of voluntary information given about medical conditions being distinctly limited. Therefore, whilst some side issues of medical conditions were not known due to no relevant medical research being available in earlier generations, there could be an unfortunate attitude amongst medical professionals that only basic essential information needed to be given.

Thankfully, however, in recent generations there has been a strong recognition of the necessity for positive communication between medical professionals and patients (parents/legal guardians where children/young people are the patients). These days I believe that it is true to state that such contact is actively encouraged, so concerns and questions can be openly expressed and asked, in order for potential side issues/problems related to medical conditions can be understood and reassurance given, both during and between appointments.

Nowadays, my parents would have been fully informed respecting side issues of both my conditions, so that such establishments as schools would be aware of my conditions and related practical needs and present or potential problems before I started school. Therefore, from nursery school upwards, teachers would know the implications of issues, and doubtlessly explain my conditions to my peers at their level of understanding,

During my first year of junior school, I was admitted to GOSH for my second palatal repair surgery. Having only been fifteen months old when I had my first operation, I obviously did not remember it, so this admission would effectively be a new experience, about which I was quite excited when I was told.

I was admitted in March 1968, and during that stay my parents experienced significant advances in children's hospitalisation compared with when I had my first operation in 1961. Whilst parental accommodation was still not the norm as nowadays, visiting was comparatively unlimited, including operation days. Therefore my mother was with me much of the time, and my father visited as much as possible, subject to work and commitments at home. (One such commitment was updating the car from an A35 to a Riley Kestrel which my parents bought from a family friend. The car was red – my favourite colour – and my father collected it in time for him and my mother to drive to collect me from GOSH so it was a surprise for me!)

When I stayed in GOSH as a toddler, I had an individual cubicle within my ward, but in 1968 I was in the main ward and the only girl for my entire ten-day stay. Whilst somewhat outnumbered, my fellow patients and myself got on well – most of the time! Being seven, I had no problems with my mother not being with me until late morning, especially as there were organised activities, including school. Obviously teaching had to be flexible due to the varied age range of patients and the length of their stays in hospital. In the 1960s, teachers visited individual wards, but in recent generations there has been a complete school within the new hospital outpatients' building. On my first day of 'GOSH school' the teacher asked me if I could do certain things within the core subjects. When I replied positively her response was, "I bet you can't!" The teacher was obviously egging me on, but, taking things literally as children do, I remember feeling most put out!

On Sunday my mother and myself attended the service in the hospital chapel, and that occasion proved to profoundly influence my entire life (see chapter four).

The next day was the day of my surgery, and being the first operation of which I was aware, I had no idea what to expect. All I had been given to understand was that I would be asleep, so would know nothing about it and wake up when it was all over, and I do not recall asking any questions about the surgery.

If I had known the reality of the pre-operative procedure of not being able to eat or drink at all, then being given what felt to me like an excruciatingly painful pre-medication injection in my bottom without either of my parents being present, I very much doubt if I would have been quite so excited at the prospect of my potential 'adventure' at GOSH!

My operation was scheduled to take place in the morning, so my parents were not allowed to visit me until the afternoon, but I clearly remember the compassion of the nurses as they tried to comfort me by telling me Teddy could go to theatre with me and that when I woke up after my operation my parents would have arrived. With such reassurance and a couple of comforting hugs, I finally calmed down and became drowsy and peaceful as I was wheeled to the operating theatre accompanied by the Teddy and the ward sister, whose gentleness I have always remembered, along with that of the anaesthetist, as I went to sleep.

The next thing I knew was being back in bed in my ward, my parents having arrived as promised.

I alternated between sleeping and waking for the remainder of the day. Knowing that my parents were with me was a great assurance, and in their turn, my parents were very glad to be with me on my operation day.

The day after my operation I got up and dressed, but recall being rather subdued and reluctant to let my mother out of my sight upon her Arrival. However, two days after surgery I was much brighter and returned to the hospital school class, which I enjoyed for the rest of my stay in GOSH, alongside visiting the GOSH playground. Overall, with the exception of the operation day, I recall quite enjoying my stay in GOSH.

One day I had a great surprise when my grandparents suddenly materialised. I enjoyed quality time with them whilst my mother went out to Oxford Street to buy me a special 'discharge from hospital' present on my grandparents' and aunt's behalf, as I discovered in due course.

When I was discharged from GOSH, we all enjoyed the ride home in our updated car. On arrival home, my parents gave me a very appropriate 'coming home present', namely a book entitled *The Golden Book of Peter Pan*, which included a chapter about GOSH due to the connections between Sir James Barrie and the hospital. The next day we went to visit my grandparents and Aunt Ruth for tea and as well as themselves, I was greeted by a large 'Walkie-Talkie' doll who was sitting on the settee wearing a bright yellow dress! For some reason, I instinctively named her Elizabeth, and she became one of my two favourite dolls of all time.

On returning to school the next week, I received an enormous welcome back from my teacher and class, having been absent for much of the Easter term of 1968 due to illness and my admission to GOSH. In my first few days, my teacher filled me in on primary points as she taught our class, and every time she stated textbook page numbers, many of the class leapt up and rushed over to show me where we were! Whilst the help was genuine, the teacher soon realised that a number of my classmates – especially boys – were 'helping' me as a valid excuse to leave their seats! Our teacher pleasantly told the class that, although it was very kind of them to help me, I really did not need everybody to show me things at the same time! Although that high level of helpfulness inevitably did not last long, I really appreciated it and the welcome back which I received.

When my generation was at junior school, daily Christian assemblies were the norm, with hymns, Bible readings and prayers. I used to always love the 'Crimond' setting of 'The Lord's my Shepherd'. (Little did I know how much my love of the hymn would be indulged when I became an organist!) However, on my return to school following my stay in GOSH, I longed for the day that we would sing 'There is a green hill far away' since that was the hymn sung in the GOSH chapel service. When we finally sang it near the end of term, it was my highlight of that day. When I told my grandparents we sang the hymn in hospital, my grandfather told me that when he was in the Holy Land during the war, the group of men whom he was with sang the hymn near the site of Calvary, so they sang 'There is a green hill not far away…'

The operation which I had in 1968 proved to be quite successful, therefore reducing regurgitation and improving my speech so that I could be understood more easily, so my frustrations lessened.

Although I did not undergo further surgery until early adulthood, I began to attend the Dental/Maxillofacial Department (DMD) at GOSH in June 1968 and remained under their care for many years. Whilst the official age range treated at GOSH is 0–16 years, it is not unusual for patients with clefts to remain for longer, because some treatment cannot be carried out until physical growth is complete.

At my first appointment in the DMD, my parents and myself met Jock Plint, the consultant, who did a basic dental inspection, thus breaking me in gently! However, two months later, I had X-rays taken and underwent my first experience of having dental impressions taken. The consultant said that I had a problem with dental overcrowding and booked me in to have six teeth extracted under general anaesthetic. The procedure was performed in the main GOSH outpatient department, with the anaesthetic administered by gas, which did not worry me at all since injections were not involved!

In perfect honesty, I recognised a definite positive aspect of multiple extractions because, whilst I do not believe that I am mercenary by nature, I admit that I relished the prospect of receiving three extra shillings' pocket money that week, courtesy of the tooth fairy!

I also attended Speech Therapy sessions at GOSH for a few years whilst I was junior school age.

My mother and myself normally travelled to London by train for GOSH appointments, but my father would drive us all to GOSH for significant appointments, such as annual reviews and appointments with consultants where serious discussions and decisions might be involved.

Some DMD appointments were straightforward check-ups, so comparatively brief, but on other occasions I had treatment and/or was asked to attend the X-ray or Medical Photography departments, which entailed extra waiting times.

Involvement with departments such as the DMD was unique, due to strong rapports which were often formed between staff, patients, parents and siblings. Because clefts affect multiple facets of oral development, such as speech, dentition and facial bone growth, treatment can only be given at definite stages from birth to early adulthood. Therefore, staff come to know patients extremely well, and take personal interest in their lives.

Because I only underwent one hospital admission for surgery throughout my entire schooling, it was possible to substantially underestimate the amount of schooling which I missed due to the number of medical appointments which I attended over the years. My parents tried to book appointments outside school hours and term time as much as possible, but absence from school was inevitable in many cases. In childhood it did not occur to me how single/half-day absences added up and the effect they might have on my education and school qualifications in the future. Therefore, I never minded being absent from school for appointments, particularly those at GOSH, since many effectively amounted to a day out in London! If my mother and I travelled to GOSH by train, appointments were usually followed by lunch and shopping or visits to various tourist attractions for reasons of education and/or leisure. Classic examples of post-GOSH visits included visiting the British Museum in order to see the Tutankhamun exhibition and the Egyptian rooms during a term in which my class was following a project on Egypt.

During the 1968 Christmas holiday, my mother and I enjoyed a festive day in London, without GOSH being the primary reason for our visit for once! Over lunch, my mother told me that from the next term, she was going to be teaching at the Abbots Langley Roman Catholic primary school. After deliberation, my genuine and serious response was to ask my mother if she was going to become a nun!

From January 1969, my mother taught in school in the mornings, then taught her piano pupils after school and in the evenings as always. Because my mother only taught part time, if I had medical appointments she could make up time by teaching a full day on a different occasion or when school concerts and musical activities involved extra rehearsals, since she was the music teacher.

Whilst medical appointments occupied much time in my parents' and my schedules, my primary school years included many happy times of which I will always have fond memories.

When my father died in 2005, numerous memories immediately came to mind with respect to various periods of life with him, many being in my junior school years, when he clearly considered his role of being my father as paramount importance in his life – even if much of it seemed to be as an unpaid teacher or taxi-driver!

As I write, my mother aged 94 is still alive, but, sadly, has vascular dementia, which feels like a living grief, as the disease gradually removes the person she really was and is.

However, as with my father, I will always know, remember and cherish the incredibly caring and positive role which she played throughout the formative, and indeed, every season of my life.

Jeremiah Ch.1v5a reads: "Before I formed you in the womb I knew you."

I feel that my parents' obvious unconditional love and pride in me mirrors that of God, who always has and will see me as I am through Jesus.

CHAPTER FOUR
A LASTING INFLUENCE OF GOSH

Let the little children come to me, and do not hinder them, for the kingdom of God belongs to such as these… And he took the children in his arms, placed his hands on them and blessed them.
(Mark Ch.9 v14b & v16)

Originally named "The Hospital for Sick Children," Great Ormond Street for Children ("GOSH") has had a profound impact on my life, from the perspectives of my medical treatment, faith and career.

As time progressed, cleft treatment centres were established in hospitals nearer to Abbots Langley. However I am grateful that I was treated at GOSH, with its rich history and the major role which it played in so many aspects of my life.

An especially strong impact which GOSH had upon me was when I was admitted for my second palatal repair surgery in 1968.

Whilst in hospital, my mother and myself attended the chapel service on Sunday 17 March. Since we were approaching Easter, one of the hymns which we sung was 'There is a green hill far away'. Not recalling singing it before, I clearly remember being affected by both the words and tune. The hymn was written by Mrs C. F. Alexander (1818–1895), who wrote many hymns in order to convey the Christian faith to children. I believe that whilst obviously written in children's language, the hymn tells the gospel message in a nutshell, and has been a favourite hymn since I first sang it in the chapel of GOSH.

I was extremely intrigued by seeing and hearing the chapel's organ, which was the first pipe organ that I remembered seeing. In reality, the organ was very small, with only one manual, a handful of stops and pedal board, but, at the age of seven, it seemed enormous and very impressive to me!

At the conclusion of the service, I viewed the organ at close quarters, told the organist that I was learning the piano and asked if I could have a play on the organ. Unfortunately, the organist refused my request, implying that I should wait until I was tall enough to reach the pedals! Whilst logical, she might well have reasoned that if she let me play, she might potentially have to allow other children to play too!

Whilst disappointed for the present, the organist gave me hope for the future, and on the way back to my ward, I asked my mother if I could learn the organ when older, and was happy to be told that I could.

My love of the organ was born on that day, and, briefly fast forwarding to 1980, once I was studying the organ, I found myself practising on the GOSH chapel organ and playing for the Sunday service whilst in GOSH for a cleft repair operation following my major oral surgery (although officially 'over-age').

I wonder how the organist that I met in 1968 would have responded if she knew how seriously I had taken her advice with regards to learning the organ, and where it led me in the course of my life.

A BRIEF HISTORY OF GOSH

GOSH was founded by Dr Charles West (1816–1898) and opened on 14 February 1852 in a converted house on the site of 49 Great Ormond Street and was the first hospital to be built in England which was exclusively for children.

The hospital initially contained two wards, both of which contained ten cots/beds and were intended to accommodate boys and girls separately. However, due to the low number of inpatients during the first few months, just one ward was used, and thus shared by boys and girls.

By late spring 1852, the word spread that the hospital was reputable, definitely helped by the first published promotional article written by Charles Dickens, and in consequence both wards were opened.

West had to overcome many hurdles prior to realising his vision of a hospital solely for children. In the nineteenth century, children were prone to cruelty and neglect, child labour being common. Children who were ill were not welcome in hospitals because they were thought to harbour infection, and children's health was generally viewed as a matter of little importance. However, the issue of children's health and care was of extreme concern to West, who actively sought to investigate and improve their plight.

West was a determined and pioneering man, who experienced significant prejudice, adversity and pressure and opposition within his life, both personally and professionally. However, he overcame barriers, became a renowned doctor and ultimately saw his vision fulfilled in the founding of GOSH.

Whilst strong and determined, West's character demonstrated much compassion, which was manifested through his holistic vision of childcare. He cared greatly about the importance of competent nursing, including emotional/pastoral care of children in addition to medical treatment.

In respect of GOSH's funding, West had many friends who supported his vision and work, including Charles Dickens and Lord Shaftesbury, who did much to improve children's welfare.

Queen Victoria became GOSH's first patron, with subsequent members of the royal family fulfilling the role in due course.

GOSH's fame as England's first children's hospital spread, and the house next door to the hospital was bought comparatively quickly, which increased the number of available beds for children's admissions.

From 1875, hospital buildings and departments increased in number as financial support allowed. Various buildings were built and then replaced as the hospital was further developed/redeveloped. There were inevitable delays and holdups in the course of the hospital's development and expansion, not least due to the two world wars and other unforeseen circumstances.

However redevelopments continued over generations. By the mid-1960s the three-and-a-half-acre site included departments such as an outpatients' department (to which other buildings and departments were adjoined), the building where the wards were located, the nurses' home and training school, doctors' residential quarters and other facilities for the benefit of both patients and staff.

Next to the hospital is located the GOSH Institute of Child Health (GOS ICH). The University College, London (UCL). GOS ICH is an academic department of the Faculty of Popular Health Sciences of UCL. GOSH and GOS ICH together form the largest concentration of children's health research within Europe. In addition to the GOS ICH, there are now new paediatric research buildings which have been built. One such building is the Zayed Centre for research into rare diseases in children, which I felt privileged to visit during a GOSH charity day, just weeks after its opening in autumn 2019.

Due to ever-increasing requirements involved in order to further paediatric research, plans for hospital redevelopment and rebuilding are almost constant. Whilst each stage of redevelopment and rebuilding within GOSH is 'state of the art' within its own generation, time does not stand still within the field of medical research and treatment, so hospital facilities need to be able to meet such needs.

GOSH was founded through charity, and survival during its first century was totally reliant on the generosity of several wealthy individuals and the subscribers who regularly donated to GOSH.

One such supporter was Sir James Barrie, author of *Peter Pan*, whose incredible support for GOSH is recorded in the next section of this chapter.

Although GOSH's redevelopment and building projects have received financial support from the government, the vast majority of the cost of the hospital's plans and building have to be met by non-governmental means in order to secure the best possible treatment and care for children and their families, from both medical and non-medical perspectives.

Such sources of funding have formerly come from the Friends of the Children of GOS and the massive Wishing Well Appeal, which began in the 1980s and was greatly championed by the late Diana, Princess of Wales.

The support of such organisations and movements have provided many updated facilities which offer practical and emotional support for patients, their parents and families, in addition to required medical care and treatment.

In recent years, the GOSHCC (GOSH Children's Charity) has been at the forefront of supporting the hospital, its staff, patients and families. GOSHCC promotes fundraising at every level, including highlighting the substantial benefits which GOSH can derive from legacies which are left by supporters of the hospital.

West's vision was a major innovation in the nineteenth century, but GOSH's present and future is the responsibility of all who care about children's health, treatment and care as West did, whether they received care from GOSH, have family, friends or contacts which require its support or simply have a heart for the cause.

GOSH – PETER PAN'S HOSPITAL

GOSH is sometimes known as 'Peter Pan's Hospital' due to the generosity and long-standing support of the author of *Peter Pan*, Sir James Matthew Barrie (1860–1937).

Barrie created Peter Pan by combining the characters of the five young Llewelyn Davis boys, who were sons of family friends and nephews of the actor, Sir Gerald du Maurier.

The story of Peter Pan was partially influenced by traumatic and challenging experiences in his own life; not least the accidental death of his older brother, which instilled the concept of children who remained children forever.

Barrie started to write *Peter Pan* in 1903 and concluded it the next year, with the first performance of the play taking place in December 1904. The play was an immediate success and was consequently performed annually, with the exception of 1939 and 1940.

In February 1929, GOSH was contemplating a major rebuilding project, for which money obviously had to be raised. Barrie was invited to join the hospital committee respecting the project, but declined the invitation because he made a rule never to join committees. However, he promised that he would endeavour to help in some other way.

Quite shortly afterwards, Barrie donated the copyright of the Peter Pan play to GOSH, due to which the hospital made him a vice-president, and when Barrie died his will confirmed the gift of the play to GOSH. This meant that the hospital would receive the royalties of all performances of the play, any adaptations and all publications and merchandise related to *Peter Pan*, although he stated that the amount of royalties received should never be revealed.

In recognition and gratitude to Barrie for his enormous support for the hospital, one of the wards was named The Peter Pan Ward. A plaque was placed at the ward's entrance which bore the inscription:

"To the never fading memory of one who loved children, Sir James Barrie, Bt. O.M., creator of Peter Pan and most generous friend of this hospital, this ward is with gratitude dedicated."

I have personal reasons for which to be aware of significant dedications to Barrie within GOSH:

*The Sir James Barrie Wing, within the former outpatients' department included the original dental and X-ray departments, with which I was extremely familiar!

*The Peter Pan Ward was the ward where I stayed when I underwent my mandibular surgery in 1978.

*Barrie's memorial plaque which is located in the hospital chapel meant/ means so much to me.

Near the beginning of this section, I referred to the poignancy of the story of Peter Pan respecting Barrie's personal experience of the mortality of children. During my vocational career as an organist and crematorium employee, very sadly but inevitably I was involved with the deaths of some children ranging from infants to adolescents. One year in the week leading up to Christmas I was required to play for the funerals of two twelve-year-old children on successive days. Just a few days later, a television docudrama was broadcast, respecting the story of Peter Pan, and the truth and implications behind some of the storyline hit home extremely powerfully.

The part which I remember most vividly was a small boy in the nursery of a Victorian house. The little boy stated that he had heard his parents talking about when he became an adult, which he did not want to do so he was going to run away. The implication was that the child would die in childhood, so the Never Land was effectively relating to children who never grew up thus maintaining their innocence while staying young forever.

As recorded in chapter eight, my childhood ambition respecting my career was to be a children's nurse (preferably at GOSH) but ultimately my aspirations to a caring career were not realised on the medical front. However, through my involvement with various branches of the funeral profession I felt that I was maintaining links with GOSH when children died as a result of life-limiting illness or disability who were under the care of children's hospitals such as GOSH. Also, when writing a thesis on 'Death and Resurrection' as part of a Christian study course in 2006, as part of my research I was in contact with medical professionals regarding children's care including visiting Chestnut Tree House, the children's hospice in West Sussex.

One lasting negative impact of GOSH which I experienced was my phobia of crocodiles and alligators which lasted from early childhood until adulthood, the origin of which was, unsurprisingly a great mystery to my parents, family, friends and even myself as the individual who was affected.

Since the United Kingdom's climate or natural environments does not attract cold-blooded animals, risks of encountering crocodiles or alligators in daily life are non-existent, but it was amazing how often they appeared in reading matter, media and even people's homes, and tourist attractions as surprise exhibits.

However, well into adulthood I suddenly experienced an epiphany moment, in which I realised that my phobia originated from GOSH due to its Peter Pan theme, the story of Peter Pan including a crocodile.

The story was portrayed throughout GOSH by artwork such as murals, so crocodiles featured quite often, and whilst artistry was of the variety found in cartoons and story books rather than actual photographs of live specimens, I was subconsciously affected by the association of crocodiles with hospital.

The insight which I received enabled me to overcome my phobia, to the point that I can now watch crocodiles and alligators in zoos and on nature programmes, and people with whom I shared my lightbulb moments fully understood its origin.

GOSH regained the full copyrights of Peter Pan from the mid-1990s until 2007, when the European Union raised the term of standard copyright from fifty to seventy years after Barrie's death in 1937. Thus, following the seventieth anniversary of Barrie's death in 2007, the more limited post-1988 royalty agreement was reactivated. (The former Prime Minister,

Lord James Callaghan had proposed an amendment to the Copyright Designs and Patent Act of 1988.) Therefore GOSH can continue to receive royalties of Peter Pan plays, adaptations, and sale of all publications and merchandise respecting Peter Pan, so that through Barrie's legacy, continual funding can be guaranteed towards the support of all children in need of the care of GOSH.

THE HOSPITAL CHAPEL

The GOSH chapel is dedicated to St Christopher and is one of the most astonishing and beautiful interiors in London. The chapel has reasonably been described as the most sumptuous hospital chapel in the country, and Oscar Wilde described it as being the most delightful private chapel within London.

The interior was designed by Edward Middleton Barry, and in its completion in 1875, the chapel was dedicated to the memory of Caroline, the wife of his cousin William Henry Barry. When Caroline died, William donated £40,000 for the building of the chapel and also provided a stipend for the chaplain, in order for him to care for the spiritual needs of impoverished children who were living in local slums.

William was the third son of Sir Charles Barry, the British architect, who together with Augustus Putin, rebuilt the Palace of Westminster. William's brother, Charles Junior, was also an architect, and took over as GOSH's architect when Edward died comparatively young. Charles Junior designed the 1893 frontage building of the hospital, which is still standing and now known as the Paul O'Gorman Building, named after a GOSH cancer patient who sadly did not survive his illness.

Built in the Byzantine style, the chapel gives the impression of being much larger than it actually is, due to the effect of the architecture and decoration.

The chapel's interior was designed with the intention of instilling Christian faith and respect in children who could not read, through its polychrome detail and utilisation of spiritual iconography. The incredible artwork found within the chapel includes murals, paintings and carvings on the walls and columns, on the ceilings and in the stained-glass windows. All depict scenes from Christ's life and other imagery which are related to children, in order to inspire and encourage all children who saw them.

Materials used within the chapel's construction include alabaster and rare Devonshire marble, with ebonised pews specifically designed for children.

Antonio Salviati's Cosmati floor is supposedly modelled on a pavement in St Mark's Venice.

The chapel was originally located in one of the oldest hospital buildings. However, because of its Grade 2 listed building status due to its beauty, it could not be demolished with the old building, but neither could it stay in its original site according to the redevelopment plans which had been made for GOSH.

In the early 1990s, the chapel was ultimately moved to a new location within a newly built part of GOSH, the project being one of the most daring challenges which had ever been undertaken within conservation engineering. The stages of the process were inevitably multiple.

Initially all the furniture and stained-glass windows were removed for repair and restoration.

Secondly, the entire chapel building was heavily braced, so that any movement could be withstood, and all inner surfaces were fully protected.

Thirdly, the chapel was underpinned onto a huge concrete raft and enclosed within an enormous waterproof box.

On completion of the preparations, with the use of greased slides and hydraulic rams, the chapel was moved to its new location inch by inch. The chapel was moved over three days, and fortunately, the project was totally successfully completed – with half an inch to spare!

The repair and restoration of the interior and furnishings of the chapel were under the care of Peter Larkworthy, the consultant conservator. Larkworthy's great-grandfather was Alfred Bell, of Clayton & Bell, who were the chapel's original decorative artists. The actual restoration work was undertaken by Howell & Bellion of Saffron Waldon.

Upon completion of the repair and restorative work, all the chapel's furnishings were placed in their relevant positions in the chapel, so that the entire edifice was returned to its former splendour.

The one substitution was the new electronic organ which replaced the original pipe organ due to its age and consequent impracticality of the cost of its potential restoration and maintenance.

Alongside a complex of new hospital buildings, the chapel was reopened by the late Diana, Princess of Wales on 14 February 1994 (the one hundred and forty-second anniversary of the opening of GOSH).

A few months following that celebration, on 1 May, a service of rededication of the chapel was held.

Whilst my first experience of the GOSH chapel had a positive and lasting impact upon my life, it was primarily from the musical perspective, although

I later realised that it also included a spiritual dimension.

I know that I possessed a faith from a comparatively young age, but after I fully committed my life to the Lord as a teenager, the interior of the GOSH chapel had a deeply renewed impact upon me.

What touched me were the many verses from Scripture which are inscribed within the chapel, especially in the Sanctuary, around the dome and within the stained-glass windows.

I was always inspired by the verse from the canticle, the Benedicite Omnia Opera, which is inscribed around the dome:

"O all ye Children of men, Bless Ye the Lord, Praise Him and Magnify Him forever." (v26)

However, the verses which are most poignant and personal for me are Simeon's words, which are inscribed within the stained-glass windows at the front of the chapel behind the altar:

"For mine eyes have seen thy salvation..." (Luke Ch.2v30a) and "To be a light to lighten the Gentiles..." (Luke Ch.2v32)

These verses form part of my testimony, because my experience in 1968 planted a seed in my heart, which later came to fruition. Once I had committed my life to the Lord, seeing those words in the chapel windows showed me that the Lord had definitely spoken to me respecting my future life on that day.

I will always be positively affected by the influence which the chapel has had upon my life, and if I am in the GOSH vicinity of London I still visit it and spend a time of private contemplation and prayer there.

I also admit to being intrigued at the fact that, with the chapel being dedicated to St Christopher and the major impact that it has had upon my life, I married a man with the surname of Christopher!

I believe that it is true to state that for many generations, Christianity and Judaism were the primary faiths which were practised and hospital chaplaincy services were virtually totally supplied by various denominations of Christianity and rabbis and representatives of the Jewish faith.

However, in recent decades/generations, the stance has necessarily and inevitably changed in order to include spiritual support for children and families of all other faiths.

In addition to the Chapel of St Christopher, the chaplaincy complex now includes a Muslim prayer room, a Shabbat room for Jewish families and a room which is not dedicated to any faith or religion – simply a room in which individuals can take time out for quiet reflection as needed.

Ministers of all faiths are available, and the chaplaincy complex is available 24/7.

St Christopher's Chapel hosts an intercession book, prayer tree and candles which can be lit.

Spiritual support is always available whenever needed. Even if families claim that they are not at all religious, in times of critical illness and/or death of a child/young person, there is a still a possibility that they might appreciate speaking to somebody who is not a member of the medical staff, such as a member of the chaplaincy.

The chaplaincy complex houses the GOSH Book of Remembrance for families to commemorate children cared for and treated at GOSH who, sadly pass away, and a book which commemorates GOSH benefactors and donors of legacies.

Whilst the chapel was primarily relocated for practical reasons respecting the redevelopment of GOSH, the present-day location of the chapel is far more obvious and accessible for people who might not wish to ask where it is, but be grateful just to be able to find it and visit for unscheduled timeout.

On the floor of the doorway to St. Christopher's Chapel, the word 'PAX' is set within the mosaics. That word is universal and, hopefully, myriad people in all generations have and will know peace through entering the chapel: staff, children, parents and families who attend GOSH for care and treatment and to support their loved ones.

As I conclude this chapter, I reiterate the impact which GOSH has had/will always have on my life from multiple perspectives as shared.

GOSH is globally renowned for its care, research and treatment for sick children, some of whom are bought to the hospital from overseas, because it is their only hope or final hope of survival.

Likewise, medical staff and students attend and access the hospital for training and pioneering projects which will potentially save and improve children's lives in the future.

Therefore, to have such an establishment within a twenty-five-mile radius of my home during my years of medical treatment and care was an incredible blessing.

Whilst redevelopments and building and research at the hospital will always be ongoing, one thing which will never change at GOSH will be its ethos expressed in its motto: 'The child first and always.'

Like Peter Pan himself, the boy who never grew up, GOSH will never stand still or age in its care for sick children.

The respective names and legacies of Dr Charles West, the hospital's founder and Sir James Barrie, one of its greatest benefactors, will never be forgotten.

CHAPTER FIVE
A ROLLER COASTER OF ADOLESCENCE

My frame was not hidden from you when I was made in the secret place,
when I was woven together in the depths of the earth. Your eyes saw my
unformed body; all the days ordained for me were written in Your book
before one of them came to be.
(Psalm 139vv15-16)

As stated in chapter two, both my parents and I were extremely serious about my being able to attend Longdean School, Hemel Hempstead for my senior school education. The primary reasons were twofold: its strong musical department and high academic standards overall. However, whilst rather less academic, Longdean offered a third attraction in the form of an outdoor swimming pool!

Longdean was a comprehensive school which was formed in 1970, through the amalgamation of Apsley Grammar and Bennett's End Secondary Modern schools, with the headmaster being Mr Valentine Wrigley, the headmaster of Apsley Grammar School.

Because Longdean was not the nearest senior school to Abbots Langley, my parents' initial application for me to attend there was unsuccessful. However, following my parents' strong appeal to our education authority, I was offered a place at Longdean halfway through the 1971 school summer holiday!

Upon receiving the welcome news, my mother and myself headed to the Hemel Hempstead schools' outfitter shop in order to purchase my uniform and, in due course, we acquired all my other requirements.

My parents and myself visited Longdean and met Mr Peter Daine, the deputy headmaster and headmaster of the lower school, and Martin Pardey, who was the first-year headteacher. Mr Pardey proved to be an excellent year head, for whom my parents and myself always held great respect and appreciation, from both academic and personal perspectives, so it was an enormous blessing that he remained at Longdean throughout my time there. Unless year heads left the school, they remained in charge of the same year group from the first year until pupils' O-level/CSE courses at the conclusion of their fifth years. Having purchased my uniform and all other necessary items, my parents sorted all essential practical issues such as travel arrangements and naming my uniform and personal possessions.

On the first day of term in September 1971, I was escorted to school by one of my mother's piano pupils, and when I joined my form, I was very pleased to meet a classmate from my junior school.

The first day at Longdean was extremely positive, with our form spending the morning in our form room with David Fisher, our form master, getting to know each other and engaging in such as tasks as writing out our timetables and completing forms respecting personal information, prior to commencing lessons in the afternoon. Not having originally been allocated a place at Longdean, I missed the first-year induction day in July, so the first day of term was the day of my initially meeting Mr Fisher and members of my form, apart from the pupils who had been at my junior school in Abbots Langley.

Transition from junior to senior school is a substantial step in the life of all children, entailing many adjustments from multiple perspectives, such as longer school days, travel if relevant, moving between various parts of the school, being taught by different teachers for respective subjects, and homework being a regular part of term-time routine.

Not living locally to Longdean, I joined the significant number of pupils who relied upon public transport in order to travel to Longdean and other schools within Hemel Hempstead. Over the years, we were often subjected to the nuisance of buses being cut out or being left behind when they were full.

My parents and myself established an after-school routine allocating time for meals, homework, piano practice and relaxation. On starting to learn the violin and joining the orchestra and choir in due course, violin practice had to be added and late arrival home from school taken into consideration. However, whilst I cannot remember how, everything managed to be fitted in!

In my first year, all pupils were taught within form groups for academic subjects, with year groups therefore only mixing for PE/games and out of class.

Forms were streamed according to ability, based upon primary school reports, and to my parents' and my gratification I was in one of three forms which were considered to be the standard of the former Apsley Grammar school.

Whilst very encouraging to know this, the form standard was very high and took a lot of living up to!

In the first year, my form had two scheduled homework subjects each day, with three at weekends. My dreaded homework days were those on which maths homework was scheduled. At junior school, my parents were informed that I was not at all bad at maths, but I found Longdean's first-year maths syllabus extremely difficult and invariably needed my father's help, he being excellent at maths. Unfortunately, I always became quickly and exceedingly frustrated when I could not understand the task in hand, however clearly my father tried to explain. Neither of us being blessed with great patience, maths homework sessions could be considerably stressful until I ultimately saw the light, so could complete assignments. I received good marks and comments for maths in school reports for classwork and homework (thanks to my father's help!) but admittedly exam results were somewhat less secure!

Whilst it was a privilege to be in the top academic stream during my first year, and although I achieved creditable assessments for classwork and homework assignments in many subjects, with the exception of music, English and geography, my first-year exam results were not wonderful – primarily due to not cultivating a methodical revision strategy. Therefore I experienced a degree of ridicule from some form members who were more able and organised in preparing for exams.

In the second and third years, whilst remaining in our forms for some subjects, pupils were placed in sets for French, maths and science based upon first-year performance, both overall and exam results.

Whilst definitely not of the ability to be in 'elite' sets, I was extremely pleased to find myself placed in sets which were of a creditable standard but where I could cope with the syllabi of subjects successfully. From the second year, the branches of science (biology, chemistry and physics) were taught separately.

During my second year, I also grasped the concept of effective revision strategies for tests and exams, and duly pleasantly surprised myself with results in all subjects. I especially thrived in French during my second and third years, much enthusiasm and progress being due to Genevieve Keech, the teacher who was French herself and with whom I just 'clicked'.

In addition, being placed in appropriate sets for core subjects, I was also in the specialist music class for the second and third years, which was both a great privilege and pleasure.

Outside lesson time, in addition to musical activities, I felt privileged to serve as a prefect in the lower school library during my first year, and during most of my third year I was a server for lower-school staff at lunchtime, which entitled me to free school meals. My parents gave me half my dinner money, putting the remainder towards the cost of the school skiing holiday in Austria in which I asked to participate.

As a server, I put my French to good use on several occasions by taking requests for after-dinner drinks. On failing to gain the attention of the French teachers when I spoke in English, I summoned up the courage to address them in French, which received an immediate response and a number of accolades – especially from my own French teacher and another master who was also French.

I also enjoyed participating in lunchtime swimming during the summer terms, outings and a couple of holidays, including the skiing trip to Austria (at the end of which I managed to pass the test – just!).

The third year of senior school was significant being the academic year in which pupils chose subjects which they wished to study for O-level/CSE courses in the fourth and fifth years in addition to the obviously compulsory core subjects of English and maths. However, in the 1970s it was not obligatory to select any of the branches of science as options.

Pupils chose an option from five standard option blocks, mine including French, history and biology.

In addition to the standard blocks, there was an extra block, which included less popular subjects such as Latin, music and RE, all three of which I should like to have taken. (My interest in Latin was inspired by my love of and involvement in church music.) However, only being able to select one subject from each block, I obviously chose music. Unfortunately, choosing a subject from the specialist block meant that there were insufficient periods within the O-level/CSE timetable to continue PE/games lessons, which I had always enjoyed despite my limited ability in sport! In addition to PE/games, I always voluntarily participated in sports days, my involvement earning me honourable mentions in assemblies and commendable comments in school reports because I always completed events in which I participated. The fact that I nearly always came last by quite a margin in every race in which I entered was irrelevant!

When I chose my options for my O-levels/CSEs, I found myself in a quandary respecting which exam course to follow in a number of my potential subjects. Apart from music, in which I was clearly capable of taking O-level and maths, in which I was definitely bound for higher-level CSE, I was borderline O-level/CSE in most subjects. Ultimately, after serious discussion with my parents and teachers, I followed the O-level course in music, French and history and CSE course for the remainder of my subjects (O-levels being entirely exam-based and CSEs being assessed on coursework and exams).

Being conscientious and wishing to achieve to the best of my ability, I preferred the prospect of being in O-level classes, because I wanted to study amongst pupils, the vast majority of whom would likely be serious about their work. I was concerned that CSE classes would include peers for whom academic success was not high on their lists of priorities, so were likely to be disruptive and distract pupils who, like myself, wished to proceed to sixth form and higher education, but CSEs were more reliable routes for us to achieve our goals. Although CSEs included exams, we could put maximum effort into coursework and thus almost guarantee high marks in that domain, which would compensate for 'mishaps' in exams.

In due course, I achieved CSE grade one in English (equivalent of O-level English language) and grade two in maths, which, whilst not quite the O-level equivalent, was regarded as a fair standard then. I also duly gained grade B in my O-level music, so could proceed to A-level English and music in the sixth form, in addition to various average grades in my other subjects.

During my five years at Longdean, I both had and made friends within my form and in other forms and years, such as members of my games group and the special music class. I also had pleasant acquaintances through mutual studies as we moved up the school in our forms, sets, O-level and CSE classes.

However, whilst I received excellent teaching and a lot of enjoyment at Longdean – especially in connection with the music department – unfortunately throughout my years at Longdean, I also experienced much unwelcome attention from some form members, and significant numbers of pupils outside my form and year due to issues related to my cleft palate. In my first year, many pupils could not believe that I was in a grammar stream form, since, having physical medical conditions, it was presumed that I also had learning difficulties, so would have been in one of the lower or lowest stream forms.

Even though speech and regurgitation issues had been improved to an extent by the surgery which I underwent in 1968, there were still clear issues, as was heavy breathing through my mouth. Further corrective surgery was apparently unavailable in my senior school years, so I had to persevere as I was. I was frequently treated as an alien and often excluded from social interaction with peers.

As stated elsewhere as relevant in this book, my parents and myself had never been told that Congenital Hypothyroidism (CH) could cause mental/emotional problems such as anxiety or depression, and Autism Spectrum Disorder (ASD) was not recognised as a condition until the early 1990s.

Therefore my parents and myself, family and friends put the emotional fragility and nervousness that I experienced and exhibited in many aspects of my life down to my cleft palate, not least frustration at not being easily understood.

Whatever the origins, my emotional immaturity made me extremely gullible. Despite the multiple ways in which I stood out from my contemporaries, I wanted to be 'one of the crowd'. However, most of my peers recognised my vulnerability, and unsupportive contemporaries took advantage of my naivety by persuading me that conforming to their views would win their acceptance. Ultimately, of course, my efforts proved futile, and cost me at least one trustworthy supporter and potential long-term friend, whose company I shunned through bullying peer pressure.

Medical and emotional reasons apart, I also stood out from the vast majority of my contemporaries due to my personal interests and attitudes, such as classical and choral music; and coming from a strong Christian background I did not swear, blaspheme or follow astrology. However, being 'different' for such reasons was never a problem and I made no apologies for such life choices.

If asked, I would always have said that I enjoyed prospects and realities of new stages in life, starting senior school being a classic example. However, whilst I stated that I loved Longdean – which I did – physical and mental/ emotional health told another story. In reality, I suffered constant stomach and emotional upsets into my second term at Longdean. Consequently, I spent a lot of time in the medical room under the care of the school matron, much to the concern of my parents, staff and, scorn of many of my form and peers.

My mother took me to our GP who found nothing untoward and sympathetically reassured us that my symptoms were due to the many changes involved with starting senior school. Whilst the doctor's diagnosis was a relief, it did not instantly solve my physical symptoms or emotional insecurity, which earned me an unwanted reputation of being the girl who was always crying! Whilst my parents wanted to be supportive, I think that they often felt understandably exasperated with me. Being honest, I was often frustrated with myself when I felt emotionally overwhelmed but could not express what was worrying me.

However, I ultimately settled and, having needed the frequent support of the school matron and supportive staff for about half of my first year at Longdean, I never required the matron or medical room for the remainder of my years there except for standard reasons such as school vaccinations.

From the age of fourteen, I developed new physical difficulties pertaining to my cleft palate. As a consequence of an adolescent growth spurt,   the appearance of my facial bone structure became clearly irregular and deformed, especially from the angle of my profile. Therefore I attracted much unwanted attention from peers and pupils of all ages both within and outside school.

My O-level/CSE years were often extremely challenging with the combination of my studies and experiencing frequent verbal abuse. I tried hard to immerse myself in my studies and apply my father's philosophy that if I achieved well I would stand out for positive reasons, but it was difficult to fully concentrate if worrying about how I would be treated outside lesson times. I believe teachers suspected that I was having problems and were watching for signs of trouble, but verbal bullying is very difficult to prove unless perpetrators are overheard and caught red-handed. Also, not wanting to potentially make things worse for myself, I did not report any incidents of bullying, but did my best to persevere whilst at school, appreciate the friends I had and the sanctuary of my home and loved ones.

Obviously very concerned, my parents asked if I wanted to change my school, but, whilst grateful to be given the option, I chose to remain at Longdean for several reasons. Initially, having commenced my O-level/CSE studies, I was concerned respecting the possibility of having to change study courses. Secondly, Longdean was an extremely good school, and I remembered the considerable effort to which my parents had gone in order for me to be accepted there. Finally, I felt that whichever school I attended, I would have problems due to my current medical issues. Therefore, if I moved to a different school during an academic year, I might struggle to settle in and make friends, and thus be an easy target for any troublemakers within my new environment.

I think that my parents were pleasantly surprised and proud when I told them my decision and my reasons for making it, and I remember feeling a sense of peace that I chose to stay at Longdean.

I became a Christian when I was fourteen, shortly before my irregular facial appearance became really obvious. Looking back, I realise how the Lord upheld me in difficult times, and it was undoubtedly He who gave me the strength to opt to remain at Longdean until I had completed my O-levels/CSEs, despite the difficult attitudes and negative attention which I received.

During the final term of my fifth year, my mother raised the suggestion of moving to a new school for my sixth-form studies, explaining that, although I would be in a new environment, I would be on a par with my contemporaries, since everybody would be in new forms and starting new courses of study.

The school which my parents had considered was the Girls' Grammar school in Watford (WGGS).

Prior to speaking to me about the suggestion of moving school for the sixth form, my mother had visited the headmistress of WGGS in order to discuss the possibility of my attending there for the sixth form. (However, my mother doubtlessly also outlined my medical history and associated problems.) When I expressed great enthusiasm respecting WGGS, both my mother and I visited the school, and met both Margaret Rhodes, the headmistress, and Beryl Rodd, who was the head of music.

I was very impressed by my visit to WGGS, and the headmistress offered me a place in the sixth form in order to study Human Biology O-level and music and English A-level, on the obvious condition that I achieved my O-level music and CSE Grade one in English.

I was extremely encouraged by the conditional offer, and as my CSE project deadlines, CSE and O-level exams approached, I continued my studies and revision with renewed enthusiasm and the incentive to achieve my required results in order to take up my sixth-form place at WGGS in autumn 1976.

My mother visited Mr Wrigley, the Longdean headmaster, in order to give formal notice that I would be moving to WGGS for the sixth form. Both Mr Wrigley and Mr Pardey, my year head, expressed their appreciation for my contribution to Longdean and said that they felt that I would benefit from a change of environment. Mr Wrigley and all staff who had taught me were very positive respecting my conscientiousness in my studies throughout my years at Longdean and implied their expectations that I would be successful in my future life.

Because I took the CSE course for the majority of my subjects, after my CSE exams finished, I was required to attend a CSE Returners course until I had completed my O-level exams. However, the course primarily consisted of non-academic/leisure classes and pursuits, so my final days at Longdean were positive, with contemporaries wishing me well, some of whom I had hardly met during my entire five years at Longdean, having always been in different forms, sets and option groups!

In due course I was extremely pleased to learn that I had achieved the exam results which I required in order to follow my planned sixth-form studies, so in September 1976 I commenced two years at WGGS.

Although my anxiety issues caused me to feel unwell a few times in my first few weeks at WGGS, overall I settled in comparatively quickly and thoroughly enjoyed my time there. I certainly sensed the Christian and caring ethos of WGGS, one of its traditions being that all years supported charities within forms each term, which combined good deeds with social enjoyment!

Whilst contemporaries soon realised that I had medical issues – especially respecting my appearance and speech – I honestly cannot remember experiencing any serious verbal bullying throughout the duration of my two years at WGGS, although I was subject to frequent abuse from pupils attending other schools who travelled on school transport.

I formed some extremely trustworthy friends whilst at WGGS in my form, subject classes and senior choir, one of whom I have remained in permanent contact.

In addition to primary subject classes, such as O- and A-level studies, the sixth-form timetable incorporated non-exam subjects, including games. One of the games options was swimming, since, like Longdean, WGGS owned a swimming pool. However, the WGGS pool was superior to that of Longdean, being indoors, so, to my joy, it was possible to swim throughout the year.

Whilst I enjoyed all my studies, after serious consideration, I discontinued A-level English after my lower sixth year. Soon after commencing A-level studies, I realised that I would need to engage in far more in-depth study than that to which I had previously been accustomed in order to succeed in A-level music. Therefore, since English literature was entirely new territory (my CSE grade 1/O-level equivalent being in English Language), I felt that I should concentrate on music, since it was my primary subject. My decision was supported by WGGS staff, although I was required to continue to study English literature as a non-exam subject during my upper sixth year.

My decision to solely focus on A-level music proved wise when I duly learned that I had gained my A-level music. To my parents' gratification, I was the first person in our family to achieve an A-level.

In spring 1976, during an appointment with Jock Plint, my consultant orthodontist at GOSH, the subject of my irregular facial growth was raised. Whilst I cannot remember how and in what context, I think that I expressed my concern that I would be subject to verbal abuse and unpleasant attitudes throughout my life due to my appearance, and believe that my concerns were taken extremely seriously. My consultant told my mother and myself that surgery was now available which could correct Midfacial Retrusion (MR), the medical terminology for irregular facial bone growth.

Whilst the surgery sounded somewhat complex and daunting, the prospect of looking 'normal' and potentially releasing me from alienation and unwanted attention was extremely positive.

My mother and myself agreed that whilst there would be no obligation to proceed with the surgery if I did not wish, meeting the specialist and hearing about the procedure would be worthwhile so I requested a referral to the consultant and in due course received an appointment for six months later.

I briefly refer to this 'birthing' appointment, having previously stated that there was no corrective treatment for MR prior to my mid-teenage years. Chapter seven concentrates on my life-changing surgery, which I believe I underwent during the latter stages of the pioneering period. Therefore I was one of the first generation to be able to benefit from such reconstructive surgery.

I requested specific prayer support whilst writing this chapter, due to the sensitive nature and difficult memories of some of its content. However, I felt it important to share some difficult experiences, in order to empathise with and encourage readers of this book who might have experienced equivalent/similar situations or know anybody who could identify with what I have shared.

I can confidently testify to the Lord's hand upon my life when experiencing particularly challenging circumstances, whether or not I was consciously aware of His presence at the time.

Whilst a Christian from my adolescence, I did not always fully understand about attacks of Satan the devil/enemy which all Jesus' true disciples will experience.

Colossians Chapter 1 v24 reads:

"Now I rejoice in what I am suffering for you, and I fill up in my flesh what is still lacking in regards to Christ's afflictions, for the sake of His body, which is the church."

Paul is rejoicing because he was bearing pain and suffering which was actually being hurled at Jesus. All who know Jesus Christ as their Saviour will experience misunderstanding, opposition and persecution in various forms. The enemy especially attacks believers in their vulnerable areas, usually when least expected. It was when my faith deepened substantially that I realised that various forms of bullying which I experienced due to medical issues would have been enemy attacks because I was a Christian by then.

Although perfect, Jesus suffered ridicule, physical and mental abuse, so knows about and understands all trials which His children experience during their lives. The Lord also empathises with and blesses them when they experience and endure difficulties because they have committed their lives to Him.

1 Corinthians Ch.10 v13 reads: "…God is faithful; He will not let you be tempted beyond what you can bear. But when you are tempted, He will also provide a way out so that you can endure it."

In this verse, I believe that the word 'tempted' can also be interpreted as 'suffering'.

As Christians, although it might be hard to remember during times of trial, if we experience attacks, it is because the enemy is afraid because he knows that the Lord is blessing and using us! The enemy's schemes can be said to serve as encouragement, since if we were not effective for Jesus, the enemy would not be bothering us!

Whatever challenging circumstances any readers of this book may experience, from personal experience, I can assure you that the Lord is ALWAYS there with you, even in your darkest place, when you might find it difficult to sense that He is present.

I end this chapter with the promise of the Lord Jesus Christ at the conclusion of His Great Commission: "And surely I am with you always, even to the very end of the age." (Matthew Ch.28 v20)

CHAPTER SIX
STICKS AND STONES

Blessed are you when people insult you, persecute you and falsely say all kinds of evil against you because of me. Rejoice and be glad, because great is your reward in heaven, for in the same way, they persecuted the prophets who were before you.

(Matthew Ch.5 vv11-12)

If an award were offered for the most untrue statement ever written, I think that a strong contender for such a prize would be: 'Sticks and stones may break my bones but names can never hurt me.'

Whether intentional or otherwise, abusive words or names can cause serious long-term damage to people at whom they are targeted.

In the New Testament, James' letter Ch.3vv1-12 speaks strongly respecting the need to control the tongue due to the serious damage it can cause, despite being such a small part of the human body.

Although James wrote his letter to Christians, his comments are relevant to all human beings, respecting potential damage the tongue can cause.

James makes the extremely serious comment that if believers speak unguardedly they are using their tongues to praise and worship God whilst judging and/or condemning fellow human beings who are made in God's image, whether or not they are Christians.

Whilst it is ideally hoped that the use of abusive words or attitudes would never be deliberate, very disturbingly, this is frequently not the case. Whether due to jealously, spite, conscious or subconscious personal insecurities, many people feel an extremely unfortunate need to belittle and react negatively towards other human beings who appear different to themselves; obvious examples being culture, race, religion and any perceived physical or mental disability or weakness, however slight or severe.

These days there is ever-increasing pressure to conform to modern trends and mindsets, 'perfect' body images and examples of celebrities and role models.

As a general rule, the youth of current generations experience enormous peer pressure, and are extremely anxious to 'fit in' and be accepted by their contemporaries. This impressionable mindset affects children of early primary school age if not younger.

I do not think that there is any doubt that responsibility for such pressure lies largely with social media and the portrayed glamorous icons and celebrities.

Myriad newspapers and magazines include reports and articles respecting children/young people who have been officially diagnosed with having clinical depression and anxiety disorders due to such obsessions, and experience ostracisation if they are deemed not to fit in with their peers.

Whilst verbal bullying will probably always be present in society, with social media commonly being regarded as part of everyday life nowadays, bullying is no longer confined to being outside recipients' homes, such as in schools, colleges, workplaces and the community.

Victims can be attacked by cyberbullies on such devices as mobile phones, laptops and iPads within the supposed security and privacy of their own private space, such as their homes and bedrooms.

Occasional subjection to verbal bullying/intimidation can be difficult to deal with, but if experience of such treatment is constant and long term, permanent damage is likely to occur.

The impact of all bullying, especially verbal intimidation, can cause mental health issues in varying degrees of severity, loss of self-worth, anxiety and depression, addictions, eating disorders and self-harm.

Victims who have felt extreme despair have attempted suicide, with tragic success in some cases.

Over many generations, countless people have experienced the ruining of their reputations and lives through the tongues of other people, whether or not claims and assertions were true.

The politician Selwyn Lloyd (1904–78) stated that more human lives/reputations were ruined by the human tongue than the number of people who were killed in human conflict, such as world wars.

I have worn glasses since the age of three, having been diagnosed as being long-sighted. Therefore I inevitably experienced being called 'Four-eyes' in my early school years, alongside other peers who also wore them. However, never being the only pupil in a school class who wore them, I do not ever recall that issue as being unduly difficult to deal with. I was fortunate that my parents could afford to buy me private frames. Thus, I looked as modern as each generation's designs allowed and was not limited to the unflattering designs of the free NHS glasses. (However I always had a spare pair of the latter in case of accidental damage!)

I was far more affected by the incredibly and extremely abusive names and attitudes to which I was subjected as a consequence of my speech and physical appearance. Due to my cleft, I experienced Midface Retrusion (MR), where a pubertal growth spurt causes irregularity in the growth of my facial bone structure, culminating in a clear facial deformity in adolescence when, like all my contemporaries I wanted to appear and feel at my best.

Whilst verbally abusive attitudes were usually expressed by peers, I did occasionally experience comments from adults, who one would have thought would know far better.

I always felt very challenged if approached and asked if I had a learning difficulty in consequence of how I sounded or looked. Because whilst it is not uncommon for people who have learning difficulties to also suffer from physical issues, it is totally wrong to automatically assume that physical conditions constitute mental or intellectual impairment/challenges

On reaching adulthood, according to individual circumstances, I found myself able to defend myself by remarking that I had a cleft palate and not a cleft brain! However, having always been impetuous and strong-willed, I often rushed about and acted in a careless manner, with inevitable mishaps which might suggest that my cleft did affect my brain as well as my palate! (I think that I still exhibit this latter trait!)

Obviously the verbally abusive attitudes to which I was subjected substantially affected my self-worth and confidence, despite my best efforts to remember and exhibit my attributes and gifts.

Although privately heartbroken at the manner in which I was often treated, my parents never showed their personal upset, and were totally supportive, as were all family and friends (both family friends and my own friends).

I was always nervous when meeting new people during adolescence, because I wondered how I would be received by them, especially if they were contemporaries.

Whilst usually reluctant to report incidents of being bullied at school, I did report somebody whose verbal harassment escalated into physical bullying, ultimately posing a risk of potential serious injury.

I remember being amazed at the seriousness with which the staff took my statement and responded to the incident. I think it was easier to deal with because a physical element was involved, where as purely verbal bullying can be very subtle and secretive.

I recall my gratification when the pupil in question approached me privately and, clearly genuine, apologised to me for all the bullying to which she had subjected me. Whilst we did not become friends, from that time we greeted each other pleasantly whenever we met.

Although I did struggle significantly with unwelcome attention and verbally abusive attitudes during my childhood and especially adolescence, I am exceedingly grateful that today's modern technology and social media did not exist in the generation when I grew up so I could feel safe and secure at home.

Whilst looking back and dwelling on the past is not overly healthy, reflection is positive if practised in order to serve as a reminder of the Lord's faithful provision in the past and encouragement that His faithfulness will continue for the present and future.

In Lamentations Ch.3 vv22-23 we read the words of the prophet Jeremiah:

"Because of the Lord's great love we are not consumed, for His compassion's never fail. They are new every morning, great is Your faithfulness." (Lamentations Ch.3vv22-23)

The specialists within the Dental/Maxillo-Facial Department (DMD) at GOSH recognised the chances of my developing MR virtually as soon as I was referred to their care in 1968. However, because such growth occurred gradually, the effects upon my appearance did not manifest themselves until I reached my teens, which is common with MR.

As previously recorded, there was no surgery to correct MR until the mid-1970s. Even when surgery became available it was not normally encouraged until individuals had completed physical growth, in order to avoid the need for the surgery to be repeated should another growth spurt cause more facial bone irregularity.

That said, DMD staff do acknowledge the fact that MR inevitably occurs during patients' vulnerable adolescent years, and corrective surgery will be performed in early teenage years if it is felt that delaying surgery will cause serious psychological harm, but in such cases, patients are warned that the (major) surgery may have to be repeated in the future.

As a Christian, the Lord has spoken powerfully to me through His Holy Spirit, and I have been particularly encouraged and challenged by passages and verses, which have proved specifically relevant for me in the course of my life as I have grown in my faith and the knowledge of God's love and Word.

One passage which I have always found very challenging is Psalm 139 vv13-16.

"For You created my inmost being; you knit me together in my mother's womb. I praise you for I am fearfully and wonderfully made; Your works are wonderful, I know that full well. My frame was not hidden from You when I was made in the secret place, when I was woven together in the depths of the earth.

Your eyes saw my unformed body; all the days ordained for me were written in Your book before one of them came to be."

Much of the psalm, written by King David, proclaims God's intimate knowledge of every human being, but all individual believers can rejoice in God's care for them personally.

However, due to being born with medical conditions, one of which affected my physical appearance, I struggled to accept myself as God accepts and loves me, but through prayer ministry, perseverance and God's grace, I am finally able to accept them for myself even if it has taken me until reaching my sixties!

For many years, United Christian Broadcasters (UCB) have produced an excellent series of daily devotionals entitled 'The Word for Today', which were written by the late Bob Gass and his wife Debby. I have used the series for many years and remember a number of devotions, due to their relevance for me on specific days. In May 2020, the theme over several days was tests/trials. Whilst I cannot recall the respective passage of Scripture, I was very inspired by one of the insights, namely "Our greatest tests become our greatest testimonies".

Being able to remain steadfast in faith in times of considerable challenge is probably one of the greatest acts of witness that believers can share.

When I struggled, I gained great encouragement from 1 Samuel Ch. 16v7b, which reads:

"The Lord does not look at the things people look at. People look at the outward appearance, but the Lord looks at the heart."

What a difference there is between the world's perception of people and that of God!

Another Scripture passage which has always upheld me is Hebrews Ch.4vv14-16:

"Therefore, since we have a great high priest who has ascended into heaven, Jesus the Son of God, let us hold firmly to the faith which we profess. For we do not have a high priest who is unable to feel sympathy for our weaknesses, but we have one who has been tempted in every way, just as we are yet He did not sin. Let us then approach God's throne of grace with confidence, so that we may receive mercy and find grace to help us in our time of need."

The passage offers firm reassurance that the Lord identifies with every trial which we undergo, having known it Himself. During our lives we will never encounter any suffering which Jesus did not experience.

In Act 3 Scene 4 of William Shakespeare's play *Twelfth Night*, Antonio speaks the lines:

"In nature, there's no blemish but the mind: None can be call'd deformed but the unkind."

Marjorie Jackson included this quotation at the start of her book *The Boy David* about the Campa-Indian baby whose face was destroyed by a disease and whom she and her husband, Ian, cared for and later formally adopted.

Masterminded by and alongside countless members of the medical profession, both in his native Scotland and the USA, Ian, a plastic surgeon, endeavoured to rebuild David's face.

In 2004, I watched the Mel Gibson film *The Passion of the Christ* soon after its release. I opted to watch it alone so as not to be influenced by reactions of other people. If specifically moved by any part of the film, I wanted to be so entirely by my own experience and understanding of what I saw.

There were comprehensive English subtitles throughout the film, because it had been produced in the Jewish Palestinian Aramaic, Latin and Hebrew languages.

The technical production of the film was excellent, and having visited the Holy Land twice, recognising the renowned biblical sites and scenery brought back special memories of the visits.

Based upon the four gospels, the film focused upon the final twelve hours of Jesus' life, and the graphic portrayal of every form of the Lord's suffering left virtually nothing to the imagination, so the film classification of 18 was definitely appropriate.

Mel Gibson must have realised that his film would be considered as highly controversial due to its graphic content. However, he wanted to produce the film as realistically as possible, in order to highlight what Jesus experienced when He suffered and died to pay the price for the world's sin. Whilst the scenes which portrayed Jesus' physical suffering and ultimate crucifixion were certainly violent, my overriding memory of the film which touched me most deeply was the portrayal of the mental, emotional and spiritual aspects of Jesus' suffering.

I was, unashamedly, moved to tears by the depiction; my emotion specifically stirred by the thought-provoking consideration that if Jesus, the sinless Saviour, suffered so much in order to pay the price for my sin, how could I as an imperfect human being not expect ridicule, misunderstanding and persecution in life. In concert with every human being, if I had been the only person to be born on Earth, God would still have sent Jesus to live, suffer and die to pay the price for my sin, such was His love for me.

The Scripture passage from Hebrews Ch.4 (previously quoted and commented upon) came to mind as I thought about the film, due to Jesus' empathy with human vulnerability through personal experience.

The entire fifty-third chapter of the prophet Isaiah foretells Jesus' suffering and death. In particular, verses 2b-6 describe both verbal and physical abuse which Jesus suffered prior to His crucifixion:

"He had no beauty or majesty to attract us to Him, nothing in His appearance that we should desire Him. He was despised and rejected by mankind, a man of suffering and familiar with pain. Like one from whom people hide their faces he was despised and we held Him in low esteem. Surely He took up our pain and bore our suffering, yet we considered Him punished by God, stricken by Him and afflicted. But He was pierced for our transgressions, He was crushed for our iniquities; the punishment that bought us peace was upon Him, and by His wounds we are healed. We all, like sheep have gone astray, each of us has turned to our own way; and the Lord has laid on Him the iniquity of us all."

In addition to the death of the suffering, passion and death of the Lord Jesus Christ Himself, in the Acts of the Apostles, we find the story of Stephen, the first Christian martyr, who was mocked and stoned to death because of his staunch allegiance to Christ. As he was attacked and fast approached death, he prayed for Jesus to receive his spirit and also for the Lord not to hold the sin against his perpetrators (Acts Ch. 7 vv54-60). What an example of faith to attempt to live up to!

I conclude this chapter with Paul's renowned words to Christians in Rome, as it is another scriptural passage of encouragement that whatever trials we face in life, God is ultimately in control.

"Who shall separate us from the love of Christ? Shall trouble or hardship or persecution or famine or nakedness or danger or sword? As it is written: 'For your sake we face death all day long: we are considered as sheep to be slaughtered. No, in all these things we are more than conquerors through Him who loved us. For I am convinced that neither death nor life, neither angels nor demons, neither the present nor the future, nor any powers, neither height nor depth, nor anything else in all creation will be able to separate us from the love of God which is in Christ Jesus our Lord." (Romans Ch.8 v35-39)

CHAPTER SEVEN
ALL CHANGE

…for I am the Lord who heals you (Exodus Ch.15 v26b)

In autumn 1976 my parents and myself met David James, the maxillofacial consultant at GOSH in order to discuss the pioneering facial surgery to which I referred to near the end of chapter five.

The appointment was very involved, and I was shocked as the consultant explained my medical issues to my parents. I realised that medical professionals considered me to have a significant facial deformity and speech impediment. I remember being quite upset after the appointment and remarking to my mother that there seemed to be so much that was wrong with me. Nevertheless, my parents and myself were very impressed with David James the consultant and the length of time and uninterrupted attention that was allocated to us.

In 1977 I attended an appointment alone with David James, when I asked my own questions respecting the available surgery and discuss any issues which were of particular concern to me. The consultant was both very pleasant and helpful, taking my concerns seriously and fully answering all my questions. I was emphatically assured that the surgery would "improve my appearance dramatically" and I gained the implication that my speech would also improve considerably.

On leaving the consultant, I met and had the opportunity for an impromptu chat with the senior dental nurse, who endorsed the consultant's assurance that the surgical procedure would definitely improve both my appearance and speech, and thus enhance my overall quality of life.

Whilst I told my parents about my discussions with the consultant and Christine, I did not immediately say that, in consequence of that day, I would wish to undergo the surgery in due course.

Late one night in March 1978 I suddenly decided that I wished to proceed with the surgery before too long. With my characteristic impetuousness, I went straight to my parents' bedroom to tell them, despite the hour. My father was asleep, but my mother woke, and in the dark, with no warning I made my great announcement!

My mother told my father my decision the next morning, and on arrival home from school that day, she told me that my father had contacted the

DMD at GOSH and that David James could see me the next day.

My appointment was positive, with the consultant and myself agreeing that the obvious time to schedule my surgery would be after finishing sixth form and before commencing higher education or career training. The consultant reiterated all that the surgery would entail and, having confirmed that I wished to proceed, I received a pleasant letter of response from him which included a choice of operation dates for autumn 1978.

Whilst under the care of GOSH for outpatient appointments and treatment, my operation was scheduled to proceed at the Royal Ear Hospital (REH), which was part of University College Hospital (UCH).

The medical name for my surgery was 'Le Fort 2 Maxillary Osteotomy'. My maxilla (upper jaw) would be broken and moved forward, its size being extended with a bone graft from my hip. This would realign my jaws and teeth, thus improving my facial appearance. My jaws would be immobilised with a small aperture for feeding and an external metal framework would be attached to my face for about two months, whilst my facial bones knitted together in their new positions, during which time my hip would also heal. Post-operative care would entail a liquidised diet, stringent oral cleaning and weekly check-ups in order to monitor progress and adjust the tension of the framework as required. Due to its circular shape, the top part of the framework was called a halo, but had no relevance to sainthood!

Once my surgery was booked, preparations had to be made including copious X-rays and impressions being taken. Splints had to be made in order to protect my teeth, since cleaning would be impossible whilst my jaws were wired together. I was shown photographs of patients who had undergone the surgery. The improvement in their appearance was incredible and a great encouragement to me as I awaited my operation. However, less than two weeks prior to my surgery date I learned that my operation had to be postponed due to a necessity for a complete technical revision for my procedure.

As previously recorded, I inherited my physical features from my paternal family. One feature was a comparatively small upper face and jaw, which caused a slight underbite (prominence of the lower jaw and teeth). However, whilst the feature was not a problem for my father (and other family members,) because my cleft palate prevented normal growth of my upper face, the combination of this factor and the family trait caused my substantially deformed facial appearance as I grew.

When planning my surgery, my consultant and team realised that the bone structure of both my maxilla and mandible (lower jaw) were significantly irregular. Therefore, it was decided that my consultant should perform a mandibular osteotomy, prior to the originally planned maxillary osteotomy, in order to ultimately achieve the best result for me. The mandibular osteotomy would involve breaking my mandible, removing an appropriate portion of excess bone and moving my mandible back, so that my chin and lower teeth would be far less prominent. The healing process would be similar to the care following the scheduled surgery on my maxilla, except that the recovery time would be approximately six weeks, with no bone graft or external framework involved. My maxillary osteotomy would be scheduled to proceed virtually immediately (or as soon as possible) following the successful completion of the recovery period following my mandibular operation.

Although this change of plan was obviously more complex than originally expected, I understood and accepted the reason for the revised recommendation. Thus, my team's preparations for Plan B began in earnest, with my mandibular surgery proceeding in October 1978.

David James, my consultant, apologetically informed me that my first operation would proceed in GOSH for practical reasons, but I was promised that I would be allocated one of the ward's side rooms. My team probably thought that being eighteen, and therefore legally an adult, I might not be pleased about being admitted to GOSH rather than an adult hospital. However, I was very happy at the prospect of having my surgery in familiar surroundings where I knew all the DMD staff.

In the week prior to surgery, I attended GOSH for pre-operative medical checks and attachment of my dental splints. On leaving the DMD after my appointment, I asked my consultant if I could eat a normal diet until my surgery now that my splints were in situ, and was informed that I could eat whatever I could afford!

When admitted to GOSH I felt a mixture of relief and nervous excitement that the day of my first operation had arrived. I had my bath and received my premedication injection (the administration of which was decidedly less traumatic than in 1968!). I recall transferring to a trolley and being wheeled from my room, then the next thing I knew was being back in my room and aware of nurses around me. On contacting my ward for information that afternoon, my father was told that my surgery had gone well and I had asked for my Arsenal scarf!

Inevitably I fluctuated between sleeping and consciousness for the remainder of that day and my first post-operative night. During that period, I was 'specialled', meaning that I received one-to-one nursing care. With my jaws wired together I needed constant attention in case I felt or was nauseous or coughed. My consultant visited me the next morning and assured me that my operation had proceeded very well.

My parents visited me in the afternoon of the day following my surgery and were amazed to see the difference in my lower face, despite post-operative swelling and bruising. A nurse standing nearby suddenly realised that I had not seen myself since my surgery and fetched a mirror. I too was astonished to see the definite alteration in my appearance, even whilst I currently looked as if I had fought several rounds in a boxing ring!

On my second post-operative day I felt much better and, with all tubes and drips removed, I was able to dress and walk around the ward. When my mother arrived, she was astounded to be greeted by me at the ward door, and was impressed by my clarity of speech in spite of my jaws being firmly wired together.

Regarding speech from the perspective of quantity, I imagine that all who knew me well, and understood the surgery that I had, must have wondered if my jaw immobilisation would put the kybosh on my verbal output for a while. If so, they were probably disillusioned! When I asked Michael Mars, one of my orthodontic consultants, to sign my 'medical' autograph book, he wrote, "We tried to stop you talking but no success!" prior to adding his best wishes and signature!

The only negative aspect of my stay in GOSH was that the catering staff apparently did not cater for patients who required liquidised diets following major oral surgery. Consequently, I was served normal meals which I had to mash and negotiate through the tiny aperture in the device in my mouth, to which wires immobilising my jaws were attached. On visiting me one lunchtime, Michael Mars was most intrigued to find me endeavouring to eat spaghetti bolognaise in that way!

My progress following my mandibular surgery was recorded as incredibly fast, and I was discharged from hospital just four days after my operation. My parents drove up to GOSH to collect me, complete with my medications, oral hygiene paraphernalia and personal possessions.

Whilst obviously happy to be home, I was inevitably very tired and in some post-operative discomfort. My parents and myself were nervous during my first week at home because, whilst post-operative oral hygiene procedures had been explained to us, we were conscious that there were no medics immediately on hand to help if we had a problem, although we could have rung GOSH if necessary. However, at my first post-operative appointment at GOSH we were reassured that we were managing well and that my recovery was proceeding as would be hoped and expected, so we felt more relaxed.

Over the next weeks, our food mixer was in constant use, as my mother prepared meals then liquidised my share, adding eggs for extra nutrition! In due course, my parents and myself enjoyed a few drinks in coffee shops. I inevitably invited amazed looks from patrons who spotted my oral device and we had to do some explaining!

With my recovery from my mandibular osteotomy apparently proceeding well, my consultant and team began to prepare for my maxillary surgery. However, to the great consternation of my parents, myself and my medical team, I contracted infective hepatitis during the recovery period following my first surgery. Consequently, my second osteotomy had to be postponed until results of regular blood tests proved that my liver function had returned to normal, and that I had recovered in myself. I was eventually confirmed fit for my upper jaw surgery from early 1979.

Nevertheless, whilst suffering hepatitis was inevitably a major setback regarding surgery, my 'health cloud' possessed a silver lining, because when I felt better, I was able to participate in activities which I would have missed had my upper jaw surgery proceeded when planned – especially Advent and Christmas activities and services. Additionally, once my mouth was free of the wires following my mandibular surgery, I was able to enjoy normal food as my family celebrated my father's birthday in early December and Christmas in due course. Alcohol was the only item from which I refrained, having been advised to completely avoid it for a year.

Once fit to undergo my maxillary surgery, the operation was booked for February 1979 in GOSH. However, whilst admitted to hospital, my operation was cancelled again due to a milk allergy, which developed as a belated side effect of hepatitis. Deliberation between medical professionals resulted in the conclusion that it would be unwise to proceed with my surgery if I could not tolerate unlimited milk, since it would be a vital ingredient in my liquid diet post-operatively, as with my first jaw operation.

My consultant must have wondered when he would ever perform my originally scheduled maxillary surgery.

However, it finally went ahead on 20 March 1979 in the REH as initially booked! When I asked my consultant to contribute to my autograph book in between my two osteotomies, David James wrote that he promised to "bone-up" before my next operation and would try not to be too cutting! Respecting 'boning up', he had plenty of opportunity, in consequence of all the cancellations which occurred due to various unforeseen circumstances!

Jock Plint, whom I knew for the longest of all my team, was equally optimistic in his contribution to my book, as he wrote that he hoped all the bones would go into the right places!

I was admitted to the REH two days before my maxillary surgery in order to allow for formalities and have my new protective dental splints fitted in the UCH Dental Hospital. On David James' pre-operative visit, we were both relieved that my 'expected' operation looked set to proceed. However, I still only truly believed that it was going ahead as I was being wheeled to the operating theatre.

I woke up in the Intensive Care Unit (ICU) pleased to realise that the long-awaited event had occurred. As following my mandibular osteotomy, my consciousness was extremely random during my initial post-operative period. Also as with my first operation, because my jaws were immobilised, stringent care had to be taken in order to ensure that I did not choke if I coughed or suffered feelings or reality of post-operative nausea. Thus a nurse was beside me practically all the time during the initial twenty-four hours following my surgery. When awake, I was intrigued by all the intravenous tubes which were attached to various parts of me, and registered the tension of the wires in my mouth and external framework which was fixed to my head and face.

When David James visited me the day after my surgery, he told me that all had proceeded as well as hoped and expected, then very kindly added words to the effect that I deserved things to proceed smoothly for once!

After four days in the ICU, I was very pleased to return to my ward in the REH, although part of the transfer was somewhat nerve-racking when, due to the REH lift being out of order, I had to be carried up the stairs in a wheelchair, complete with my external framework causing me to resemble a sci-fi character!

In total I stayed in REH for over three weeks, during which time I greatly appreciated the support and contact of family, friends and neighbours, with at least one of my parents visiting me every day. The constant travel to/from London must have been exhausting on top of work and commitments at home. Whilst I obviously thanked them, I hope that my parents realised just how much I really appreciated them.

My discharge from REH was initially deferred due to a haemorrhage in my hip, from which bone was taken in order to form the graft in my maxilla. On hearing of the setback, an elderly great-aunt expressed her concern in a letter to my parents. Written in literally correct and intended perfectly innocent phrasing, the exact wording read, "I am sorry to hear that Katy's bleeding hip put her back in bed!"

Unfortunately, my second scheduled escape was also thwarted due to another totally unexpected problem respecting my framework, which had to be realigned and strengthened under general anaesthetic, Consequently I had to spend another couple of days in the ICU because of having to be put to sleep again.

When finally discharged from REH in mid-April, our food mixer was back in regular use! As after my lower jaw surgery, preparing my food and oral hygiene were daily priorities for my parents and myself.

Returning home during Holy Week, I much appreciated being able to watch all the Christian programmes and services over the Easter weekend. I also requested a chocolate Easter gift to be able to enjoy in due course!

As with my mandibular osteotomy, television provided a significant source of entertainment during my recovery following my maxillary surgery. Being springtime, viewing included the usual extensive coverage of the World Snooker championship which my parents and myself enjoyed. 1979 was the one year in which Terry Griffiths won the championship in his first year of qualifying to play at Sheffield. Coming over as an extremely pleasant man as well as a great player, Terry Griffiths became my snooker hero. I wrote to him to thank him for entertaining me following surgery, and duly received a reply, which included an autographed photograph.

My recovery period also included the 1979 general election, when Margaret Thatcher became the first female United Kingdom prime minister. The day after the election, my mother and myself watched the television coverage, being joined by our GP at one point. My mother requested a home visit because a wire on my oral device in my mouth was loose and sticking into me! The duty doctor proved to be one of our favourites, who patiently twisted the wire with the end of a teaspoon in the very limited space in my mouth to the background of political activity and excitement from parliament!

My parents drove me to weekly check-ups at GOSH, since travelling to London by public transport with my external apparatus was not an option. Check-up appointments were generally straightforward, ensuring that progress was ongoing and that my framework and the device in my mouth were secure and as tight as possible without causing excessive discomfort, and my parents and myself were able to raise any issues of concern.

Whilst I did not suffer too much discomfort from my operation or apparatus during my nine weeks of recovery from surgery, there was a week when I did experience considerable pain which unfortunately was particularly triggered by laughter. When an episode of *Fawlty Towers* reduced me to tears of agony instead of laughter, I had to limit myself to serious reading and viewing matter until my next check-up, when I duly told my consultant about the acute pain which I had experienced in the past week whenever I had laughed. David James' initial 'helpful' advice was to watch the news instead! Seriously, all my medical team were extremely concerned and sympathetic about the amount of pain which I had suffered that week, and double-checked all my apparatus in efforts to prevent, or at least minimise, such discomfort in future.

Had my team seen me two days later, when Arsenal dramatically won the FA Cup final during the final minutes of the match, I think that their primary concerns would have been for the survival of my oral appliance and external framework!

With my maxillary osteotomy occurring in the spring, longer days and pleasant weather enabled me to appreciate short local walks, rides and sitting in the garden. Sporting my external framework and oral device, when outside our home during my weeks of recovery, I deliberately looked for and was very amused by reactions and responses of people, since I obviously looked somewhat extraordinary! My favourite incident concerned two young girls who saw me as they passed our front drive and garden. Whilst the girls did not initially stop, I think that my contraption caused them to do a double-take behind our hedge, and they suddenly reappeared and very politely asked me to explain what I had on my face! My mother and myself explained and the girls went on their way. I would love to have known what they told their families about me!

My framework and oral device and wires were finally removed in late May 1979 and, true to David James' promise, my face did not collapse in a heap on the floor! My mother said that for such assurance to be volunteered, a patient must have asked if their face would collapse when their framework was removed!

My parents, myself, family and all who knew me well were totally astounded by my new facial appearance.

I immediately made hairdresser and optician appointments, and duly emerged looking much tidier and proudly wearing the new stylish glasses to which my parents treated me.

Whilst wonderful to eat normally again, I built up from soft food, until before long I could enjoy completely normal fare. I then belatedly consumed my large Lindt chocolate Easter rabbit!

However, whilst my osteotomies did wonders for my appearance,

My Father, Frank Semper (13) with my paternal grandmother, Ida

My Paternal grandparents Ida and George Semper

Mother, Beatrice, aunt Ruth & maternal
grandparents Tom & Ivy Hart

My parents wedding day with both sets of parents

Mother's bridesmaids; Aunt Ruth & Father's cousin, Jean Massey.

Parents and myself at 4 months

Shortly after my first birthday

A performance in my earliest days of piano tuition with my mother

Early career considerations-nursing or music?

Promotion to the Junior section of 1st. Abbots Langley Girls' Brigade company 1967/8

During a four-day break to Paris with my mother 1975

One of the original Great Ormond Street Hospital buildings in the
nineteenth century.

New main entrance to GOSH

Foyer of redeveloped/redeveloping GOSH

New GOSH main entrance

Zayed Centre, one of the newest research buildings opened in 2019

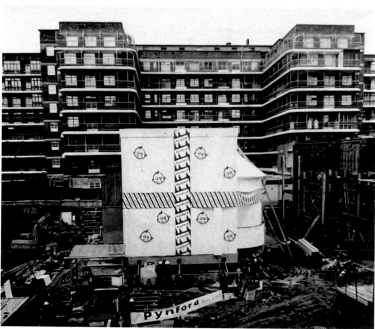

Relocation of GOSH's chapel from an original building into the main hospital

Memorial plaque in the chapel

Interior of the GOSH chapel

A stained glass window which meant much to me

Original pipe organ in the chapel- which inspired my love of the organ.

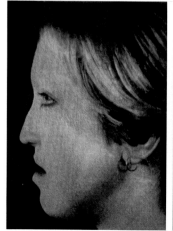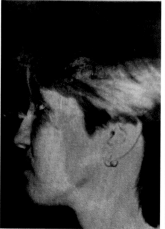

These diagrams are examples of my profile before/after my oral surgery in 1978/79.

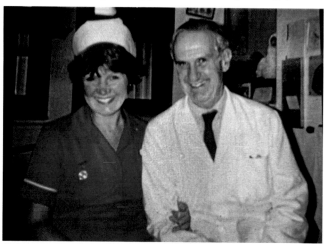

Christine Godber, Senior Dental nurse, & Jock Plint, Consultant Orthodontist GOSH.

Michael Mars, Consultant Orthodontist,GOSH

David James, Consultant Maxillo-Facial surgeon. GOSH/UCH

Sunbathing in "Star Wars" mode following my maxillary osteotomy May 1979.

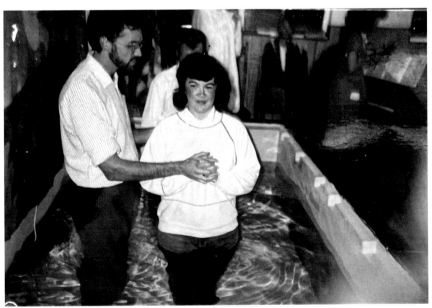

Baptism at Ingatestone Elim Pentecostal Church October 1st 1989

A.(Cert.)CM Presentation, Lambeth Palace 1st November 1989.

Graduation at Colchester Institute School of Music 4th November 1989.

Wedding of Hugh and myself 16th July 1994.

At reception venue with Best Man, Roland Christopher, and bridesmaids:
Fiona Christopher, Clare & Janette Shepherd and Felicity Bell

Hugh's parents, Joan & Syd Christopher

My parents' Ruby Wedding anniversary 10th August 1997

Hugh, myself, my mother, Hugh's brother sister-in-law and family 2018
(Sarah, Fiona, Roland & Anna)

A favourite realistic image of myself (taken by our niece Christmas 2019.)

Silver Wedding Anniversary of Hugh and myself

Sixtieth birthday photograph of Hugh and myself 2020 (delayed due to Covid 19)

and thus my self-confidence, unfortunately they were not the final oral operations which I required. In moving my maxilla forward, a residual cleft from childhood reopened, which necessitated further surgery. Expecting my osteotomies to be my final surgery which was related to my cleft palate, the reality of requiring yet more surgery was a major shock, although I later discovered that such circumstances were not unheard of.

I underwent two operations which were performed by a consultant plastic surgeon UCH/GOSH in 1979/80. However, due to post-operative and personal issues, I decided that I needed a complete break from surgery for a while, so I settled for wearing a dental obturator which prevented regurgitation and aided my clarity of speech.

During that period, I gained my first employment in the Civil Service whilst pursuing organ studies and private music teaching at home in my own time.

In spring 1983 I considered the possibility of undergoing further cleft repair. Through musical activity my mother and myself knew a local family where one of the sons had been born with a cleft lip and palate. As a young adult, the son had undergone palatal repair surgery, which was performed by Ronald Pigott, a consultant plastic surgeon at Frenchay Hospital, Bristol. The young man and his family were delighted with the result and highly recommended the consultant to my parents and myself.

I asked my GP for a referral to Ronald Pigott and received an appointment to meet him in due course.

My mother and myself attended the appointment and we were extremely impressed by the consultant from both medical and personal perspectives. I think that my GP wrote an extremely supportive referral letter for me because, judging by the way that Ronald Pigott spoke to us, he obviously understood the complexity of my medical history, and sympathised with me with respect to the difficult medical circumstances which I had experienced.

In due course, I attended Frenchay in order to undergo a nasoendoscopy. The procedure was performed by the consultant himself, enabling him to see the condition and functioning of my palate. Feeling very comfortable in Ronald Pigott's care, I asked to undergo palatal repair surgery at Frenchay, which proceeded in autumn 1983.

Being a distance from home, I knew that I would not have many visitors, so ensured that I took plenty of occupations to Frenchay with me. In addition to books and writing materials, I took a few volumes of organ music since, prior to admission, I had asked for and received permission to practice the organ in the hospital's chapel and a church near Frenchay, once

I was well enough to get dressed and go out following my operation. My parents and myself were extremely impressed with the treatment and care which I received in Frenchay hospital, and Ronald Pigott's surgery was very successful, so proved to be my final surgery related to my cleft.

Since undergoing my reconstructive facial surgery in early adulthood, what I have most appreciated is the fact that I no longer stand out negatively in society due to my appearance and speech; a blessing which I will treasure for the rest of my life. I enjoy meeting new people and am confident about exchanging basic greetings and/or passing relevant comments with people whom I do not know. The vast majority of people appear to understand me on the assumption that I remember to speak slowly and clearly!

Some months following my osteotomies, I learned that my parents had attended a private appointment with David James, my consultant, in order to discuss the surgery in my absence, and ask his advice as to whether they should actively encourage me to undergo the operation if/when the subject arose. Apparently my parents specifically asked if the surgery would bring my upper and lower teeth closer together, because they were well aware that my underbite was considerably pronounced.

The consultant's response was that whilst the surgery might enable my teeth to meet, and my top teeth might even overlap my lower teeth as is normal, in all honesty he could not completely guarantee that. However, the consultant said that he could promise that the surgery would definitely realign my jaws sufficiently to ensure a considerable improvement in my appearance and speech.

In actual fact, my consultant was able to move my maxilla sufficiently forward for my upper teeth to slightly overlap my lower teeth, a fact about which my parents and myself were absolutely delighted. Whilst a cleft resulted which required further surgery, ultimately all the benefits of my reconstructive surgery outweighed related problems.

My lower jaw will always be larger than my upper jaw, but my mandibular osteotomy considerably reduced its size and prominence. Therefore, following my maxillary osteotomy my jaws and teeth were in far better alignment, consequently presenting me with the invaluable gift of an essentially normal facial appearance.

The consultant declined payment for my parents' appointment, stating that they had been wise to meet with him privately so that I would not discover that they had visited him without my knowledge.

David James, Michael Mars, Jock Plint and Christine Godber, the GOS senior dental nurse, were extremely significant people in my life for many years, from both professional and personal perspectives. I have always been very grateful that they formed my primary team throughout all the treatment which I received from childhood through to early adulthood, especially regarding my osteotomies.

Upon completion of treatment, I was assured that I could always contact them for advice if I ever had any concerns about issues which were related to my treatment, and I was grateful to be able to do so on occasion.

Jock Plint passed away in 2011, and in the process of carrying out my research for this chapter and the Medical Addendum near the end of my book, I was very sorry to learn that both David James and Ronald Pigott had also passed away in comparatively recent years. Whilst I did not know Ronald Pigott for nearly as long as all my team at GOSH, I greatly appreciated being under his care in the early 1980s. I shall always be grateful that I knew and treated by those medical professionals and treasure their memories.

All members of the medical profession whom I knew well are also acknowledged in chapter ten, in which I express appreciation for all through whom God has blessed me in various spheres and seasons of my life.

When I first considered the available reconstructive facial surgery and all that it entailed in 1976, it sounded somewhat drastic! However, forty-plus years on, nine weeks of recuperation, liquidised food and resembling a Star Wars/science fiction character was so brief, when I think of the benefits which I have known since then, especially from a psychological perspective.

Whilst such surgery was not lifesaving it was definitely life-changing. Without it I very much doubt if my life would have developed as it has, from the perspectives of higher education, profession, spiritual and social fulfilment. Although I ended up having two reconstructive operations instead of one, in retrospect I feel it was appropriate that I had the surgery which I initially expected in spring 1979 as Easter was approaching, because as Easter signifies new life through Jesus' resurrection from the dead, the surgery which I had provided me with a new physical life, the benefits of which I would/will reap for the remainder of my earthly life.

Whilst not for spiritual reasons, I can honestly state that I wore a halo and literally had a screw loose on more than one occasion in consequence of the medical paraphernalia which I modelled for about two months!

Whilst the Lord knew and loved me as I was from conception, He also knew and provided the physical healing which I would require in due course and provided it through the skills of the medical profession.

CHAPTER EIGHT
CAREER MAKES AND BREAKS

I know that there is nothing better than for people than to be happy and to
do good while they live.
That each of them may…find satisfaction in all their toil.
This is the gift of God. Eccl.Ch.3 v12,13b)

From infant-school age, my ambition was to be a nurse and keep music as
a serious hobby. My resolve never wavered, and when I was seventeen
I applied to the nursing schools at GOSH and Westminster, which is now
Chelsea and Westminster.

However, I was informed by the GOSH school of nursing that they held
a policy not to accept long-term GOSH patients as student nurses, because
they were likely to experience difficulty in adjusting to being nurses after
having been patients. Therefore, such applicants were strongly encouraged
to apply to hospitals where they were not known in any way.

Whilst understanding the logic of the policy, I expressed my immense
disappointment, because it was my treatment at GOSH which had inspired
me to pursue nursing as a career, and I had my heart set on ultimately
working with the babies and children who had been born with clefts as I
was. In consequence of my appeal, I was invited for an interview at GOSH,
but was declined an offer of a place on a course.

Nevertheless, my application to the Westminster hospital was successful,
and I was accepted on one of their training courses, although I ultimately
never took up my place due to unforeseen circumstances which resulted
from my facial reconstructive surgery.

Still, my heart remained set on a medical career which was relevant to
my own experiences, because I felt that I would be able to empathise with
patients. Therefore, during 1980 I considered the possibility of becoming
a dental nurse, with the aim of eventually working in a dental/maxillo-
facial department. I researched dental nurse training and was offered six
weeks' work experience in a local dental clinic. Being encouraged by that
experience, I applied for and was accepted on a Dental Surgery Assistant
(DSA) training course commencing in March 1981 at the Eastman Dental
Hospital (EDH) in London.

The course lasted a year followed by six months' employment as a qualified DSA at the EDH. Regular practical and written assignments were required and students received assessments respecting their work and progress in the various departments of the EDH. An intermediate examination was held after four months, which comprised of a written paper and viva voce, and was considered to be equivalent to O-level Human Biology standard.

However, whilst I found fulfilment in engaging in empathetic care of patients, practical aspects of the course proved to be very challenging for me; one prime example being my struggle with the dexterity necessary to handle extremely thin and delicate instruments.

As the first months of the course proceeded, I gained high marks in written assignments and duly passed the intermediate examination. Unfortunately, however, my practical assessments from most of my departmental placements clearly showed that I would not be able to achieve the standard required in order to qualify at the end of the course. Therefore I was regretfully informed by the Principal of the DSA school that I could not remain on the course. However the hospital continued to pay me for the full first half of the course on account of the fact that I had passed the intermediate exam.

Whilst I was very disheartened by the news, I duly learned that such situations were not unheard of.

When I told Jock Plint, one of my orthodontic consultants at GOSH, what had happened, he responded that whilst sorry that my hopes had not worked out, I had not committed too much time to a profession to which I was not suited to. The consultant told me that occasionally medical students experienced equivalent experiences to those which I had encountered, but because they did not work on wards/with patients until the third year of training, they would be unaware of any problems until they had successfully completed two years in medical school. Therefore, they would inevitably experience a significant sense of loss of time, and great uncertainty regarding their future, having channelled all their hopes and studies towards their ambition of pursuing medicine from senior school years or even earlier.

I remember fully comprehending Jock Plint's comments and, thereafter, found myself increasingly wondering if my experience at EDH was a sign from the Lord that I would have experienced similar problems and duly discovered that nursing itself would not have been an appropriate career for me.

However, no opportunity is wasted and I was always satisfied that I had tried a medical career.

After leaving EDH, I did not find further full-time employment in 1981, although I found a couple of temporary jobs and continued my organ studies and teaching at home.

Consideration of non-medical employment required some mental adjustment, having finally accepted that a medical-orientated career was not appropriate for me.

In early 1982 I found temporary employment in the Civil Service (Watford Tax Collection), which I quite enjoyed, the flexible working hour system and income enabling me to continue my organ studies and private teaching in my own time.

I was originally offered a place to commence a diploma course at the London College of Music in autumn 1982, but I was unable to take up my place because diploma courses did not qualify for mandatory grants and I could neither secure a discretionary grant or afford to self- finance.

Instead, during summer 1982 I succeeded in securing a permanent position in the Watford Tax Inspector's office (HMIT). I must have been the most reluctant civil servant ever employed when I first started there, having been forced to decline my place at music college.

However, as with my previous Civil Service employment, the flexible working hours, pay and income enhancement of my private teaching enabled me to continue and finance my organ studies.

During my years of working in the HMIT I underwent my final cleft palate surgery in 1983 and succeeded in passing my driving test (at the fourth attempt!).

In time, I came to appreciate my years in the Civil Service, formed positive working relationships with many colleagues, and joined in events run by the social club.

However, from 1985 I decided to pursue professional music training and left the HMIT in 1986, in order to commence my degree course at the Colchester Institute (see chapter two).

Following graduation in 1989, I should have liked to have been able to concentrate solely on music, but due to freelance work taking time to build up I resumed combining clerical work with playing the organ and private music teaching.

Not finding any vacancies in the Civil Service immediately after college, I secured employment in the X-ray department of Watford General Hospital for a year prior to locating and applying for a vacancy in the Watford DSS office in summer 1990. Following a successful interview, I was reinstated as a civil servant and remained in the DSS until 1994 when Hugh and myself married and I moved to Lancing.

Overall, my years in the DSS were the happiest that I spent in the Civil Service. In addition to clerical work, I found opportunities to be involved in roles such as switchboard duty, which I found extremely rewarding, because I felt that I was helping people through direct contact rather than behind the scenes.

As always in the Civil Service, the flexible working hours were very beneficial because I could build up hours to use when I was requested to play the organ for midweek services such as funerals rather than having to take annual leave.

In addition to playing for services and teaching, I also resumed some organ tuition in order to keep my hands (and feet) in, although I had to travel further afield for lessons since my original teachers no longer taught in Watford.

I enjoyed good working relationships with many DSS colleagues, some of whom became long-term friends. One such person was one of the DSS management staff who interviewed me for my Civil Service reinstatement, then four years later conducted my wedding with Hugh (see chapter twelve).

Once married and living in Lancing, Hugh supported my ambition to build up a freelance music career, which combined organ playing and private music teaching.

Having moved to a new geographical area, building up my career obviously took time, since I had to publicise my name and availability. I did so through contacting churches and crematoria in Worthing and Brighton, and advertising in Yellow Pages, libraries and shops. I also joined the Incorporated Society of Musicians (ISM), which promotes and supports qualified musicians in every area of the profession.

In time, I was increasingly contacted with requests to play in crematoria, chapels and churches between Worthing and Brighton. Although crematorium work was not contracted full-time employment, requests for my services snowballed as clergy and funeral directors whom I met at crematoria requested me to play for them at their respective churches and individual venues (such as cemetery chapels).

I also built up my private music teaching practice to an upper limit of twenty pupils because my freelance career combined both teaching and playing.

I also received many requests to play for Sunday services at churches other than Lancing Tabernacle ('Tab') where Hugh and myself are in membership, but I limited these to a few specific local churches, so that I was normally able to attend the Tab at least once on Sunday. I was generally requested for morning services when 'playing away' because many churches did not hold regular evening services.

Respecting crematoria, whilst I regularly played at Worthing crematorium for a period, and at both of the Brighton crematoria, Woodvale and The Downs, I was an organist at Woodvale for twenty-four years, then from 2008 became increasingly involved with all aspects of crematorium work until 2016.

Within this chapter, I refer to my involvement in the funeral profession in the course of my freelance career as a whole. However, the next chapter focuses entirely on my years of involvement at Woodvale Crematorium, and the substantially positive impact which that participation had upon my life, together with the influence of so many crematorium colleagues, clergy/officiants and funeral directors. Whilst freelance work can be less financially secure than contracted permanent employment, I experienced enormous gratification in being able to fully concentrate on music for a considerable number of years, prior to my freelance work leading into surprising new avenues of ministry.

I refer to my career from 1994 onwards as a vocation/ministry because I firmly believe that it was the Lord's leading and perfect timing that I became involved in such avenues once Hugh and myself settled in Lancing following our marriage.

Ecclesiastes Ch.3 v1 reads:

"There is a time for everything, and a season for every activity under the heavens."

Whilst I mostly travelled for playing the organ, I taught most of my pupils at home, although I reserved one day per week to teach at homes of pupils within the geographical boundary of Worthing who could not easily travel to Lancing.

I taught pupils from the age of six up to adults, my subjects being Piano, Jazz Piano, General Musicianship, Theory and Aural. I also accompanied instrumental examination candidates, both those who were my own pupils and students of other teachers.

I taught theory and aural to my own pupils as an integral part of their regular lessons, with extra separate coaching for examinations if necessary.

However I also taught those disciplines to students of different teachers as separate subjects if required. A prime example was students who wished to achieve their grade five Theory of Music exam, which was a prerequisite of one music exam board in order to proceed to the top three practical exam grades (six–eight)

I prepared pupils for the pre-grade one Preparatory Test, examinations from grades one to eight and the Performance Assessment, in which students can prepare their own programme of pieces and receive a certificate comprising the examiner's constructive assessment. Such assessments were very helpful for any students with special needs, or preparing for top grade exams where the individual and myself considered that an 'interim' professional assessment would provide a clear indication of progress to date.

Obviously I neither could or did not insist that my pupils prepare for examinations, although many opted to do so. However some pupils were adamant that they solely wished to learn to play the piano so that they would be able to play their choices of music for their own pleasure and relaxation.

I admit that preparing pupils for examinations was extremely rewarding, from the first stage of helping pupils choose their exam pieces through to the day of the exam itself (that is on the assumption that candidates put in the sufficient amount of practice between lessons!).

In pupils' final lessons prior to exams, I always hoped to be able to state that they played to the examiner as they had just played to me so they would do themselves justice. Definite highlights of teaching included informing pupils that they had passed their exams, then discussing the result in the next lesson.

When I first began to enter pupils for exams, I expressed concerns to my mother that examiners would question my teaching if pupils made mistakes in their exams about which I had constantly commented in lessons leading up to the exam. I recall my mother's reassurance that all examiners were either former or current teachers, so they would have experienced the same exasperations and concerns which I felt!

During my years of teaching, many pupils achieved merit and distinction category marks, but, on the assumption that they passed, I praised my pupils heartily irrespective of the category of pass – unlike a certain teacher formerly mentioned in chapter two! Whilst I was obviously very pleased when pupils passed exams, primarily it was their success.

I taught some pupils who took music at GCSE and A-level and proceeded to study music at university or college and it was a pleasure to hear of their graduations and ongoing success in due course.

Inevitably during my teaching career, I had a few pupils who did not achieve the exam pass mark at their first attempt for understandable reasons, ill-health on the day, excess nerves, an extra-strict examiner, or a combination of all the above! Of that small number, most pupils retook and passed their exam the next term or sometime later. However, one or two, having originally wished to enter for the exam, did not realise how much practice was required in order to pass even the first exam, or did not heed my repeated instructions and advice, so therefore the unfortunate outcome materialised!

Because neither of my practical instruments are orchestral and private teaching could be solitary, I always appreciated chances to associate with other teachers and members of the music profession. Such association could occur through the ISM, which held courses in various aspects of the music profession, accompanying instrumentalists for exams or other occasions, giving consultation lessons and miscellaneous social interaction with musical friends and colleagues. Involvement with church music and worship groups is another prime example of mutual interest.

Occasionally I was contacted by people in order to ask if I could recommend teachers for various instruments from personal contact or experience.

My most memorable such experience was when I was contacted by a gentleman who had seen my teaching advertisement in the Yellow Pages and wanted to ask if I knew a colleague who could teach him to play the bagpipes. The gentleman's initial phraseology implied that he was asking me to teach him, and he sounded extremely aggrieved that my advertisement did not include the bagpipes!

Seeing that I had struggled to play a descant recorder due to my cleft palate, I never contemplated learning any other instrument which involved blowing – except for the pipe organ, for which sound production I was not personally responsible!

In response to a few polite questions, I finally ascertained what the gentleman was trying to ask me, and whilst I could not help him, at least I was satisfied that I had understood him enough to try!

As my mother had done, I arranged annual pupils' concerts at home, although they were not large events such as my mother's had been, not least because I never taught as many pupils as her due to teaching not being the only area of my freelance career.

I discontinued teaching once my involvement at Woodvale Crematorium increased in 2008 but retained records of the progress and standards of all my pupils, both in Hertfordshire and West Sussex, and value the memories of them all. I always cared about all aspects of my pupils' lives in addition to their learning music with me and, because the vast majority of my pupils were of school age, I kept up to date with term/holiday dates and latest crazes, Hugh and myself never having had children of our own.

Since retiring in 2016, I have frequently felt satisfied when recalling my career. I feel gratified to consider that, whilst I started regular work later than average, I managed to secure contracted permanent employment of various kinds until the Lord led me into the position where I was able to fully commit to building my freelance career.

I can genuinely state that I gained positive experiences from all avenues of my career from practical, confidence and spiritual perspectives.

CHAPTER NINE
DEATH DUTIES

...If anyone serves, they should do so with the strength God provides, so
that in all things God may be praised through Jesus Christ.
(1 Peter Ch.4 vllb)

Prior to being involved in the funeral profession, both as an organist
and member of staff at a crematorium, I hardly associated the above
field with drama and almost unbelievable anecdotes. However, after many
years' such experience, I firmly believe the saying 'You couldn't make it up!'.
Many incidents were highly embarrassing at the time, but contained a
funny side, which I could appreciate later, even when they were at my
own expense.

I refer to my involvement and role in the profession as a vocation/ministry
because I firmly believe that it was the Lord who led me into this field, and I
look back upon those years as some of the most fulfilling of my life.

From autumn 1994, I was a member of the team of organists at Woodvale
Crematorium, Brighton, and I also played at churches and chapels between
Worthing and Brighton.

Whilst inadvisable to become over-emotionally involved when
participating in so many funerals, I never felt it possible to be sensitive to
the ambience of funeral and thanksgiving services without participating in
spoken parts of the service as well as fulfilling my role as the organist.

I had always aspired to a career in which being involved with caring
for people was a primary role, hence my original ambition to be a nurse.
However, as my participation in the funeral/bereavement field materialised, I
realised that I was involved in a caring profession, albeit in a different sphere
to my original intention. I felt immensely privileged to be a member of a
profession which helps people at an extremely difficult period in their lives,
regardless of the circumstances of the death.

However, there are inevitably particularly traumatic circumstances of
death which occur, including the death of infants, children, young people,
homeless, and victims of suicide and violence.

I was always moved by funerals of people who died with nobody or very
Few to mourn for them, especially if they were comparatively young. In
such cases, funeral directors and pall bearers would sometimes sit in the

services, and when I later became a full-time member of crematorium staff, if circumstances permitted, I would do likewise.

Soon after starting to play at Woodvale, a colleague told me that, even if professionally involved in bereavement, it would be unnatural to feel totally unmoved by especially poignant circumstances of death and funerals. Throughout my years there I was always influenced by the manager's comment that there is only one chance to get everything right for a funeral and that is at the time. Any errors will potentially add to the family's grief and stay with them forever.

Once involved in the funeral profession, whenever I attended funerals as a mourner, I realised the importance of all funeral professionals' roles, so when I returned to my professional role, I always felt a fresh commitment to my vocation. Also, through my ministry my appreciation for my own family and friends substantially increased.

However, as stated at the beginning of this chapter, despite professionals' best efforts, unexpected events can and do occur which can affect all personnel within their respective roles.

When I joined our parish church choir in 1973, the vicar was Rev. Canon Ron Martin, to whom he and his wife Elsie I was extremely close, from adolescence through to their deaths within just three months of each other in 1989.

On retiring in 1977, Ron and Elsie continued to live locally, and Ron conducted many funerals at the crematorium near Watford. When I visited, Ron told me many anecdotes regarding his experiences. Whilst I greatly enjoyed Ron's stories, I admit that I did not believe half of what he told me. However, once I played the organ and was involved in the funeral profession, I remembered and believed everything!

One intriguing aspect of being a crematorium organist was the diversity of repertoire. In many cases, recorded music was played for 'unusual' requests, but sometimes it fell to the organist to play items which were not normally associated with 'religious' services,(which most services were when I first started playing regularly at crematoria).

If requested to play for funerals in church, organists normally received a minimum of a week's notice, enabling time to locate sheet music and learn the requested items, but when playing at crematoria and cemetery chapels unique requests could sometimes be made with as little as twenty four hours notice. Personal experience of such requests which I experienced included the Hallelujah chorus from *Messiah*, 'We'll keep a welcome in the Hillside', 'The sun has got his hat on' (requested as entry music on

Maundy Thursday) and 'Always look on the bright side of life'.

This last number was intended to be played on CD, but the disc was accidentally left in the hi-fi system at the family's home. With no crematorium CD available it was all down to me. The Woodvale office presented me with downloaded sheet music immediately prior to the start of the service, and I found myself silently practising it on the organ manuals in competition with Queen songs and the spoken parts of the service. Fortunately, my 'party piece' had been requested as the exit music, which gave me the maximum time for preparation. To my relief and joy, the family and all staff were very positive in regard to my eleventh-hour performance.

Although I had been playing at Woodvale for a while at the time of the above occasion, somehow I had escaped 'Always look on the bright side of life', which was/is one of the most popular music choices for crematorium funerals, alongside 'We'll meet again', 'The white cliffs of Dover', 'Somewhere over the rainbow' and 'My Way' sung by Frank Sinatra.

However, it was extremely important to remember that, however unusual a musical request, or how often organists were required to play hymns such as 'Abide with me', All things bright and beautiful' and 'The Lord's my shepherd' (Crimond), all funerals were unique occasions for families.

I always approached every service I played for as if it was the only service that I was playing for on that day, even when playing for multiple services which often happened at the crematorium.

Unfortunately, in recent years organists are being requested to play for funerals far less frequently, especially at crematoria, because most such establishments now possess very modern computerised music systems, so that families can choose any musical track performed by any artist, and even when hymns are requested to be sung, many families opt to sing to recorded music rather than requesting an organist to be booked.

Regarding unexpected circumstances which can occur, there are three personal experiences which I think that I will remember to my own dying day.

Firstly when playing for a service in a cemetery chapel, an electrical fault occurred following the entrance music and first hymn. The fault being silent, the problem only manifested itself when the second hymn was announced and my attempt to play the introduction failed to produce any sound. After a couple of fruitless checks, the vicar and congregation proceeded to sing the hymn unaccompanied and, with the exit music unable to be played either, the vicar and funeral director led the pall bearers and mourners out of the chapel in deadly silence – literally.

Secondly, a vicar who was conducting his first service at Woodvale pressed a switch underneath his lectern in the North chapel, intending to close the curtains at the committal. Unfortunately, what he actually did was to relay his service into the South chapel, in which I was playing for another service. Thus, the vicar in the South chapel was reading a Bible passage, when he was suddenly interrupted by a loud blast of organ music from the North chapel. Everybody naturally turned towards myself as I sat at the organ, very startled and embarrassed. Thinking it might be a fault on my organ, I quickly turned the organ off and lifted my hands and feet well clear of the manuals and pedal board. However, a few minutes later, there was another loud contribution from the organ in the North chapel, and the funeral director in my chapel dashed forward into the vestry at a speed of which no staff thought he was capable! I only turned my organ back on once the next hymn was announced and thankfully, there were no further interruptions.

Once both services finished, the source of the problem was detected by chapel staff and funeral directors involved with both services. I was officially exonerated of blame, with the incident and staff's fears of my suffering a coronary being reported to the Woodvale office!

However, my most embarrassing experience occurred at a crematorium other than Woodvale, when personally requested to play for the funeral of a lady, whose daughter I knew.

The chapel was a small family chapel with insufficient room to house a permanent organ, but if required, a keyboard on a stand could be set up, which is what happened on that occasion. On entering the chapel, I immediately stated that the keyboard was situated too near to the catafalque. However, the chapel attendant emphatically informed me that it was always placed in that position. Whilst still unconvinced, I felt wary about not disputing further because I was a visitor. Thus having ensured that I would not be directly under the catafalque's curtain track, I reluctantly accepted the attendant's word.

The service proceeded smoothly until the committal, when, having heard the tributes to the deceased, I felt that the hymn 'Just as I am without one plea' would be appropriate to play, and duly began to do so as the minister spoke the committal words and the catafalque curtain began to close. Drama began at this point because, having checked that I was not positioned under the curtain rail, what had not occurred to me was the weight of the curtain. Therefore, as it moved, the strong velvet folds knocked straight into the side of the keyboard, sending it spinning to an angle of about forty-five degrees away from where I was seated on the stool. Miraculously, I managed to prevent the keyboard from crashing onto the floor. By doing a rugby tackle, I succeeded in swivelling it back into position with one hand, whilst continuing to play the hymn with the other. However, my relief was short-lived as the curtains finally came to a standstill with a further jolt albeit less forceful, so I was able to replace the keyboard for the second time, with less problem.

Only afterwards did I register what the minister and congregation witnessed. At the most serious part of the service, family and friends' farewell to their loved one was distracted by the precarious posture of the organist as she frantically tried to retrieve her instrument. With each verse of the committal hymn ending 'O Lamb of God, I come', my choice of committal music came very close to being relevant for myself as well as the deceased.

I later learned that the crematorium staff had watched the proceedings on the television monitor behind the scenes with bated breath! I also learned that the minister had not been impressed with the chapel attendant's attitude and, seeing the potential calamity, had indicated to a mourner sitting at the end of a row to jump up and assist me if necessary!

Mercifully, all present, many of whom I knew, saw the funny side. I was invited back to the family home for refreshment, of which I felt in dire need! I was very relieved to return to Woodvale in due course, with both its permanent organs being situated well out of harm's way!

I possess books by organists respecting their experiences, to some of which I can personally relate, and all the others I fully believe however incredulous they sound!

In 2008, my involvement at Woodvale increased very suddenly and unexpectedly. The Lord spoke to me through two positive comments respecting my ministry at Woodvale. Both comments were made within the same week, one by a member of our church pastoral group, and the other by a member of Woodvale staff. The encouragement which I received from those remarks reminded me afresh what a privilege it was to be involved at Woodvale, and led me to seriously explore the possibility of becoming involved in aspects of work at Woodvale in addition to playing the organ. Having seen a couple of other organists serving as relief chapel attendants, my initial thought was to request to train as a chapel attendant, so I could join my colleagues in that role as required when permanent Woodvale staff were on leave.

I shared my thoughts with a few Woodvale staff, including the colleague who made the positive comment and asked for their honest opinion as to whether they thought my idea might be viable. Everybody to whom I spoke was positive and encouraged me to speak to the Woodvale manager. In due course I was extremely gratified to learn that crematorium staff were willing to give me the opportunity to try, which was an answer to prayer in itself. I began to train in June 2008, initially observing the duty attendant then performing duties myself under supervision and finally 'flying solo'. Chapel attendant duties included preparing chapels prior to services, operating the music system and tidying up the chapels and removing coffins from the catafalque at the conclusion of services.

Once colleagues and myself felt that I was confident in the role, my supervisor told me that the next time a relief attendant was required I would be given the opportunity to take on the duty. As I left Woodvale that day, I thanked a colleague for his support. My colleague's response was that I was most welcome, and that it was in Woodvale's best interest to help me as one day I would be helping them.

I will never forget that comment for the most poignant of reasons: the next day one of the organists, who also served as a relief chapel attendant, suffered a fatal heart attack, and consequently from that week I became a part-time crematorium employee in addition to continuing as one of the team of organists. Apparently, staff commented to each other how extraordinary – even eerie – it was that I had asked to train as a chapel attendant when I did, so was sufficiently able to fulfil the role unsupervised just when our colleague died so totally unexpectedly.

When I considered what had happened, I realised that it was definitely the Lord who had led me into my new situation over the previous few months, from the encouragement I initially received to the completion of training. Nevertheless, I inevitably felt somewhat stunned by the sudden turn of events.

As time went on, I increasingly became 'part of the furniture' at Woodvale Crematorium.

In autumn 2008, the onslaught of a serious flu epidemic was forecast for the coming winter. Thus national crematoria were urged to recruit additional members of staff to train as relief crematorium technicians. That would ensure that there would be sufficient staff available to work shifts around the clock, if the epidemic materialised and caused death rates to soar and necessitate such action.

The Woodvale manager asked me if I would be interested in being one of the trainee technicians.

I felt extremely privileged to be approached and accepted the challenge.

Whilst cremation is definitely the preferred form of committal at the conclusion of funeral services nowadays, the actual process is not something which most people care to think about.

However, as in all areas of involvement at Woodvale I felt that it was a privilege to perform such a service, and represented an extension of 'end of life' care for the deceased and their families. I believe that all staff endeavoured to perform the cremation process with maximum dignity, care and consideration with which we hope that our loved ones and ourselves would be treated.

There is an official 'Cremation code of practice' to which all cremation technicians are obliged to strictly adhere. Any member of crematorium staff found guilty of breaching the code of practice would be in immediate serious trouble.

Although the flu epidemic ultimately never occurred, my cremation training meant that as long as a qualified technician was present in the crematorium, I could be included on the technicians' rota.

In due course I was entered for and passed the Crematorium Technician exam. The exam involved prepared written work and a multiple-choice exam including science and technology, and a practical demonstration of the candidate's ability to carry out all stages of the cremation cycle competently and safely. I gained much satisfaction in preparing for my exam and greatly valued the excellent tuition and encouragement of my supervisor and colleagues.

Passing the exam was a classic example of my being able to achieve any goal on which my heart was set, even if it might appear beyond my natural ability, since I did not consider science and technology to be amongst my academic strengths.

Having passed my exam, I was offered a permanent contract as a full-time member of Woodvale Crematorium staff. I felt extremely gratified that I gained permanent employment at the crematorium where I was trained and where so many colleagues believed in and supported me.

I just could not believe what those original encouraging comments had led to back in April 2008.

As I write, Barry, the church member who made the comment, went to be with the Lord very recently. Barry was a strong believer in both the positive and negative effects that the power of words can have on people. Barry's encouraging remark to me proved his point, and I ensured that he, his wife and family knew the lasting impact that it had on me.

Once I was a permanent member of Woodvale staff I rarely played the organ, because balancing the two roles could be quite difficult. However, being on site meant that I was available to play if an organist was required at short notice.

Having related a few unexpected incidents which I experienced as an organist, I have to state that unpredictable incidents also occurred respecting chapel duty; normally related to the absence of or malfunctioning CDs or mishaps regarding the 'joys' of modern technology!

As a chapel attendant, my most memorable experience for embarrassing reasons was a service which included both organ and recorded music. Having played the entrance music and first recorded music to be listened to during the service, I loaded the next CD, set it on the requested track and pressed the pause switch. The pause switch on the music system was slightly loose, so sometimes it would trip, which resulted in the CD playing before time. That was not a problem, so long as the master volume control was turned down to zero. However, on this occasion I had unfortunately neglected to turn the control down after playing the previous track, and, inevitably, Murphy's Law prevailed, in that this was one of the occasions when the pause switch tripped. Consequently, the singing of 'All Things Bright and Beautiful', accompanied by the organist was suddenly overruled by Cliff Richard's enthusiastic rendition of 'We're all going on a Summer Holiday'!

Sitting in the vestry, I listened aghast, as the singing faded out and turned into gasps, chuckles and finally full-blown laughter. The occasion was extra-embarrassing because the congregation was so large that some people were standing outside the chapel with outside speakers switched on. Therefore they and other people and staff who were nearby were privy to the sudden change of music genre.

Having stopped the CD as quickly as possible in my state of shock, the hymn resumed, and the remainder of the service proceeded without further drama.

At the end of the service, whilst the vicar was shaking hands with the congregation as they left the chapel, I sat in the vestry with much trepidation as I awaited the reaction of the vicar and funeral director.

In reality, the family asked the vicar to give me strict instructions not to worry at all, because their relative had a wonderful sense of humour and would have loved the incident. Apparently, the family themselves also thought the event was hilarious and an extremely fitting send-off for their loved one.

With that assurance, I allowed myself to appreciate the funny side, as did the vicar who conducted that memorable service, and all Woodvale staff and funeral director colleagues who unavoidably heard the proceedings, courtesy of the outside speakers!

However, in future I treble-checked that the CD master volume was set at zero until musical items had actually been announced, and there was no repeat of such events when I was on chapel duty.

As a general rule, I found colleagues within the funeral profession were a special group of personnel with whom to be associated, whatever their roles. It would probably be impossible to be involved in a profession primarily connected with death and bereavement without elements of humour and light-hearted banter behind the scenes.

However, I strongly emphasise that in front of house, all services and people are treated with the utmost professionalism. I should hate to believe that I ever seemed immune or insensitive to grief which families and friends experience. Since my involvement in the profession, personal bereavements highlighted the responsibility which funeral professionals hold to provide the best possible service.

In 2013, the Lord both gave me a vision and provided me with the financial means to create a website through which Christian members of professions and volunteer groups which were relevant to funeral and bereavement fields could contact and support each other, such as requesting prayer if involved in especially poignant circumstances. For example, funeral directors/staff and clergy who were or are called to arrange and conduct services where the circumstances of death were/are particularly traumatic. The website and email addresses are included at the end of this book, on the page which lists contact details of organisations to which I have referred in the course of my story.

I really praise God for being able to be involved in such a profession.

In Ecclesiastes Ch.3 v13, the writer states that to find satisfaction in toil is a gift of God.

It was with enormous regret that I was obliged to retire from Woodvale on health grounds in 2016.

However, the vocational fulfilment which I experienced during my many years of involvement at Woodvale will always remain with me, as will memories of many colleagues, some of whom are now long-term contacts and friends of both Hugh and myself.

CHAPTER TEN
COUNTING MY BLESSINGS

The Lord has done great things for us and we are filled with joy."
(Psalm 126 v3)

Whilst 'red letter' days of life such as birthdays, weddings, anniversaries and successes hold special memories, recollection of 'everyday' life can be equally precious. I designate the first part of this chapter to sharing my appreciation of blessings of both special and ordinary life events.

Of all the important events in my life, the most special have been my marriage to Hugh, my graduation and the many occasions relevant to my Christian faith and my graduations

I have always been grateful that my parents witnessed such highlights of my life, particularly my wedding to Hugh. With both sets of parents and ourselves marrying at older ages than average, the fact that all our parents were present at our wedding was absolutely wonderful.

Although born with two specific medical conditions, my overall health was never affected. Therefore, I have always led an active and fulfilling life, in which I was able to participate in (or at least attempt) all pastimes in which I was interested. Obviously all these interests were in addition to my musical activities, on which I exclusively concentrated in chapter two. My primary physical interests have included swimming, badminton, table tennis and ten-pin bowling, which I appreciated for the dual purposes of exercise and socialising. During childhood, adolescence and early adulthood up until early adulthood I also enjoyed horse-riding, ice- skating and roller-skating.

In recent years I have taken up keep-fit and walking which I enjoy with like-minded groups, family and friends, but also undertake alone in order to regularly maintain health and fitness. When out walking I feel extremely blessed by the fact that Hugh and myself live near the South Downs and the sea; both of which are prime examples of God's wonderful creation. I especially love being near the sea, which to me is symbolic of God's love - ever present even though it extends far beyond the horizon of physical sight.

Both of my parents enjoyed participating in a variety of sports, interest in some of which I inherited.

Swimming was the sport which all three of us thoroughly enjoyed from my earliest memories, with coastal holidays being amongst our favourites so we had unlimited access to sea-swimming.

Although I was not gifted in sport, especially as my father was, I enjoyed achieving my best sporting results in swimming, such as gaining my mile distance certificate and bronze personal survival award during my senior school years.

Indoor pursuits include reading, sudoku, crossword and codeword puzzles, murder mystery and period drama on television and Scrabble which I play with Hugh and a close friend on a regular basis.

Holidays were times of special enjoyment, both with my parents, then obviously Hugh in due course.

Destinations included both the UK and abroad, with especially memorable holidays being spent in the Isle of Wight and Benidorm with my parents (the latter being my first holiday abroad in 1972).

In addition to our honeymoon in Paris, Hugh and myself greatly enjoyed holidays in Austria, Cyprus, Ibiza, Israel, Malta and Majorca with a Christian organisation, visiting some destinations twice.

The organisation was All Age Christian Ministries, which was begun by a forthright Welsh evangelist. Whilst on a family holiday in Majorca, the evangelist Glyn Morgan sensed a need for Christians holidaying abroad to be able to share fellowship, and investigated possibilities, which became realities in due course.

The first holiday week took place in Alcudia, Majorca, with about five hundred people from around the United Kingdom taking over a hotel at the end of the 1990 summer season. Following the enormous success of several holidays in Alcudia, the ministry expanded significantly, with holidays being arranged in Holland and Lake Como in addition to the aforementioned destinations.

Holiday weeks enabled participants to enjoy hotel and resort facilities, and coach tours to the popular tourist attractions, whilst enjoying Christian fellowship with each other.

Hugh and myself met in Alcudia in autumn 1991 and when we married, Glyn Morgan and the ministry team sent us a wedding card which was read out at our wedding reception.

Hugh and myself also made friends with other participants, one couple with whom we maintained fairly regular contact since also first meeting them in Alcudia thirty-plus years ago.

The particularly special element of those holiday weeks was the ministry, which consisted of daily morning meetings and evening rendezvous. Early morning prayer meetings were held most days, and communion was normally shared during the morning meeting on Sunday.

Holiday weeks had specific themes, about which Glyn Morgan would speak on various aspects in each meeting; examples being Lord's Prayer, Beatitudes,

Living for Jesus and The Holy Spirit. During visits to Israel, talks concerned applications to Jesus' ministry respecting biblical sites which were visited.

During most visits to Israel, a number of participants were baptised in the River Jordan, an experience which was really special for them and also moving for all who witnessed the occasions.

A special achievement of the ministry was many visits which were made to Israel. In due course, Glyn Morgan received a special award from the Israeli Tourist Board which the ministry used, in recognition of the fact that he had led fifty Holy Land tours.

As the ministry's name suggested, ministry team leaders and participants represented most age ranges and worship traditions. There was plenty of opportunity for fellowship, with quizzes and competitions being organised by the ministry team on some evenings, and an in-house variety show often taking place on the last evening.

Very sadly the ministry ended in 2009 when Glyn Morgan passed away comparatively suddenly as a result of cancer, but we remember those holidays with much pleasure.

Within the UK, special destinations for holidays and breaks include cathedral and historic cities, such as Cambridge, Oxford, Gloucester, Hereford and Worcester. One favourite part of the UK is Yorkshire, with its dales and moors, rural villages and cities, especially the city of York, where we usually stay.

I feel very blessed to consider the many pleasures of earthly life such as I have recounted.

As James says in his book, "Every good and perfect gift is from above..." (James Ch.1 vv17)

Having dedicated my autobiography to Hugh and my parents, I devote the second half of this chapter to acknowledging many people who have made positive impacts upon the many spheres of my life.

FAMILY

I emphasise my enormous appreciation for the unconditional love and acceptance which I have always known from my own family and Hugh's side of the family in due course. As recorded in chapter one, my immediate family was small but I had an extended family to some of whom I was and remain very close.

I was blessed in knowing three out of my four grandparents. My maternal grandparents lived until my early adulthood and living just half an hour's drive from them and my Aunt Ruth, my parents and I saw them a great deal. My paternal grandfather went to the Lord suddenly when I was four, but living quite locally, he was a regular part of my life and I remember his fun nature and generosity towards me.

Unfortunately I never knew my paternal grandmother, who went to the Lord at a comparatively young age in consequence of serious illness. Whilst my father rarely shared personal feelings, he did express his sadness that his mother never met me, and I believe that he struggled with the fact that neither of his parents saw me grow up to the age that my maternal grandparents and aunt did.

I was told that I would have got on extremely well with my paternal grandmother as she had a great sense of humour and loved practical jokes, as did my maternal grandfather. As I grew, I displayed my inheritance of those traits and also the ability to talk for England!

When Hugh came into my life, and we duly married, we regularly saw Hugh's parents, Syd and Joan who lived comparatively near to us. Also, living locally to Hugh's brother Roland, wife Fiona and family and being involved in the same church, we saw a lot of them. Hugh and myself enjoyed seeing our twin nieces grow up. Anna and Sarah were just nine months old when Hugh and myself began courting, and never having had direct descendants in my immediate family, I considered my 'auntie' role as an immense privilege. Hugh and myself are extremely fond and proud of Anna and Sarah and all their achievements.

Thus, Hugh's side of the family became a further extension of a loving family which I have always been blessed to have known. I honestly cannot imagine how my life would have been without such a loving family network. I genuinely feel deeply for individuals who do not know such blessings.

Whilst Hugh and myself did not have our own children, we have always experienced much pride and joy in having many children in our lives.

In addition to Anna and Sarah, we have many official and honorary nieces, nephews and godchildren through family and friends. Also, through various mission organisations and charities, we are privileged to have been able to sponsor children who live in countries in Africa and Asia.

FRIENDS

Among my large collection of fridge magnets I possess a few which bear quotes respecting friends, one being 'Friends are the family we choose for ourselves.'

In the course of my life, I have been blessed with many friends, whom I met through education, music studies and activities, employment and

Christian fellowship. Hugh and myself remain in contact with some such folk whom we regard as lifelong friends.

During childhood and adolescence, I had an number of trustworthy and supportive friends, one particularly close friend being Anji, whom I met in the sixth form at Watford Girls' Grammar School in 1976. In addition to the interests which Anji and myself shared, such as senior choir and leisure sports, Anji, together with her parents and family, was incredibly supportive towards me respecting my medical issues. I will always feel extremely grateful for Anji's friendship and unconditional acceptance of me both prior to and during the entire process of my reconstructive facial surgery.

Regarding music studies and activities, I made many acquaintances through music studies and activities in Watford, Colchester and Royal School of Music (RSCM) courses over many years, some of whom became lasting friends and contacts.

Within this number I include my two organ teachers in Watford, John Winter and David Brindle, Sara Burgess and Elaine Goh, who were students at Colchester Institute School of Music. These people have been a great blessing over many years and as spouses and children came onto the scene, Hugh and myself have appreciated such long-term contacts. We have known much pleasure in following the lives of our friends' children as they grew up. Throughout my years of employment, I made long-term friendships and acquaintances, especially through working in the Watford DSS office. Such people included Paul Tucker, through whom I became involved in the Baptist church in Kings Langley, several supervisors and many colleagues with whom I had a positive rapport.

I made a significant number of friends and contacts through my freelance music career and employment at Woodvale Crematorium, on which I focused in chapters eight and nine. However, I briefly refer to such respective friendships and working relationships here, due to the blessings which they were in my life, upon which I am focusing in this chapter.

Regardless of the avenues of life in which I gained trustworthy friends, like family, I never take them for granted. True friendship is a gift from God, and there are many people in society who find both establishing and maintaining lasting friendships difficult or even impossible for various reasons, quite possibly through no fault of their own, such as mental health.

MEDICAL PERSONNEL

In previous relevant chapters, I acknowledged branches of the medical profession who treated me for my congenital medical conditions and related issues. I expressed gratitude to specific specialists by name and paid tribute to those who are no longer alive.

However in this chapter I express gratitude to all other fields of the medical profession who I have required assistance from more than average, due to my complex medical history.

I specifically acknowledge GP surgeries with which I have been registered long-term; namely, the Vine House Surgery in Abbots Langley, Hertfordshire and the Ball Tree Surgery in Sompting/Lancing, West Sussex.

I express my appreciation for the substantial support which I have always received from clinical and administrative staff at both surgeries whenever I need it.

I also record gratitude for treatment and support of all dentists, pharmacists, opticians and other avenues of medical expertise from which I have benefitted during my life.

It is very easy to take health-related professions and services for granted, especially in the Western world where such help is readily available. Being able to access such support without having to seriously consider practical availability or cost is an indisputable blessing.

Whilst never having experienced instantaneous healing for my medical conditions, I believe that it is true to state that the Lord has healed me through the skills that He gave to all medical professionals who have treated and supported me in the course of my life. I also feel that as the evolution and ongoing advance of medical science and discovery is miraculous, it is the Lord who enables it, since He alone is the Creator of all that is good.

CHRISTIAN LIFE

In acknowledging fellowships and people who have positively influenced me in my Christian life, I have listed churches in chronological order of participation there. In the majority of cases I refer to people I met there, together with respective members there to whom I was close.

In many cases I refer to people collectively due to a practical issue of space, although I do individually name pastors, church leaders and tributes to memories of people now with the Lord.

ABBOTS LANGLEY BAPTIST CHURCH (ALBC)
Early childhood–1973

I regularly attended ALBC from early childhood until early teenage years, during which time I participated in all children's and youth activities, such as Junior Church, Girls' Brigade Bible Class, youth club and Holiday Bible Clubs, in which I later participated as a helper.

The ALBC minister during my years of attendance there was Rev. Wilfred Driskell, whom I remember as an extremely godly and gentle man with a strong pastoral heart, who was always a source of personal encouragement to my parents and myself.

My parents and myself always recalled and appreciated the prayerful support which we received from Rev. Driskell, his wife, family and many members of ALBC during my years of medical treatment, both whilst I was attending the church and when I gradually became involved in St Paul's Church, Langleybury, ultimately entering full church membership there.

ST PAUL'S CHURCH, LANGLEYBURY (StPL)
1973–1986

I became involved with StPL through family friends who encouraged me to join the choir, so played a significant role in my participation in Christian music throughout my life. In 1988 I became godmother to my friend's daughter when she was christened at St Pauls.

As previously stated, when I first attended StPL the vicar was Rev. Canon Ronald (Ron) Martin, who with his wife Elsie was extremely musical. Ron and Elsie, David Anstey and Barry Judge, the directors of music in my earliest years at StPL were extremely supportive to me in my adolescent years and when I underwent my major oral surgery in my late teens. They were also strong mentors to me respecting my serious interest in organ and church music. Sadly both David and Barry passed away comparatively young through sudden illness, but I will always treasure their memories and the positive impact they had on my life. Ron and Elsie had retired by the time I underwent my surgery and began to learn the organ, but continuing to live in Kings Langley I remained in close contact with them until they passed away in the late 1980s.

Ron's successor, Rev. Gerald Drew, came to StPL in autumn 1978, and he, his wife Jane and many of the congregation were very supportive to me and my parents during my reconstructive surgery, Gerald personally travelling to London to visit me on several occasions. I also received a great deal of encouragement from everybody at the church when I began to learn the organ, and, in due course play for services for a number of years, in addition to participating in non-musical roles at the church, such as being a member of the church council.

Hugh and myself remained in long-term contact with many friends whom I made at StPL over the years, and we maintain contact with people who still attend there, although many people have inevitably both moved and passed away.

When my father passed away in 2005 his ashes were buried in the StPL Garden of Remembrance and his name inscribed in the Remembrance book in the church. My mother has requested the same arrangements for when she passes away. Thus, StPL will always be special, as I recall my parents' and my involvement, and the memories of many special people there.

ST. NICHOLAS' CHURCH, ELSTREE (StNE)
1985–1993

I became involved at StNE through a friend and fellow organist. I became the deputy organist early in 1985, initially playing on one Sunday per month, and sharing weddings and funerals with the official organist.

Whilst I had served as a deputy organist at StPL for several years, I could not be appointed as the organist there because the organist also had to be responsible for choir training, in which I had no experience at the time that the church was seeking to appoint a new organist.

The rector during my years at Elstree was the late Rev. Dr William Elliott (Bill), who was always extremely encouraging respecting both my musical participation at Elstree and personally.

The prospect of involvement at Elstree gave me the motivation which I needed to pass my driving test, because Elstree was not easily accessible by public transport, especially on Sundays.

My driving tuition up until then had previously been rather spasmodic to say the least, with intermittent instruction from two instructors, my parents and three failed tests behind me. However, the incentive of attaining an official organist position worked wonders, and I passed my test on my first attempt with BSM, following three months of thrice-weekly lessons. Having passed my test, I could fill a larger role at StNE, and in due course was appointed the official Organist and Director of Music there. Additionally, I was also able to fulfil practical elements of my church music option placement at the church, the rector serving as my mentor and supervisor.

In addition to Bill Elliott always being an extremely supportive rector, I also acknowledge the encouragement and friendship of his wife, Angela, and a number of church members at StNE.

Although Elstree was not an evangelical church, there were members at Elstree who were of the evangelical persuasion, and it was with them that

I formed the strongest relationships.

After eight years of positive participation with StNE, I terminated my involvement with them in autumn 1993 so that Hugh and myself could spend most of our weekends together as we prepared for our wedding the following summer.

I cherish many happy memories of StNE. The beautiful leather music case with which the church presented me as a leaving gift is still in excellent condition and remains a tangible reminder of the special season which I spent at that church.

CHRISTCHURCH BAPTIST, KINGS LANGLEY (CCB)
1990–1994
I was in membership at CCB from 1991–1994, my connection with the church evolving through a manager at the Watford DSS where I worked following my graduation from Colchester (see chapters eight and twelve). I received an extremely warm welcome from the minister and entire fellowship. Whilst I enjoyed fellowship with people of all ages at CCB, my closest friends there included members of the church music group and Nomads' Housegroup (so named because venues alternated between homes of all the members!).

When Hugh and I began courting in 1992, we naturally visited each other's churches when possible, and met each other's respective friends.

Once married, when visiting my parents in Abbots Langley, we always attended services at CCB and met up with our friends from there, with some of whom we still maintain contact. Unfortunately such attendance finished after my mother moved to the care home in Worthing, following the onset of vascular dementia in 2016. However my season spent at CBB was extremely blessed and encouraging.

LANCING TABERNACLE ('THE TAB')
1994–Present
The Tab is the largest fellowship to which I have belonged, and has always been blessed with the faithful ministry of the pastor and eldership, our current pastor having recently completed his first year of ministry as I write.

Lancing Tab is affiliated to the Fellowship of Independent Evangelical Churches (FIEC) and Sussex Gospel Partnership (SGP), with its activities accommodating all age ranges, both on Sundays and during the week. The church is very outward-looking respecting involvement and practical witness within Lancing itself, and also exercises a strong focus on local, national and global mission.

Both Hugh and myself consider ourselves greatly blessed to be in membership of an extremely loving and vibrant fellowship.

I refer to avenues of participation with which Hugh and myself are involved in chapter twelve, which contains a significant proportion of my testimony.

LANCING METHODIST CHURCH (LMC)
1995–2019

I have greatly valued my involvement with LMC over a significant number of years, my association with the church initially evolving through playing the organ for monthly Sunday morning services and additional occasional services as required. However, in due course I spent a period in membership at LMC (see chapter twelve).

LMC showed great love and care to both Hugh and myself, and I express sincere appreciation to LMC ministers with whom I experienced extremely positive rapports and personal encouragement; including Ronald Upson, Keith Edwards and especially Andrew Reed, with the latter of whom and his wife Hugh and myself have been pleased to maintain contact on occasion.

Hugh and myself established friendships and acquaintances with many members of LMC, although a significant number have now passed away. However I/we treasure the memories of such people, including several gentlemen who could be referred to as 'elder statesmen of the church' who both strongly encouraged and influenced me.

I will always appreciate the important role which LMC played in my life from musical, spiritual and personal perspectives.

I have acknowledged above churches in some detail, having been closely involved in them for significant periods of time, and gained many blessings band positive influences from them. However, there are other churches and fellowships which have also impacted my life extremely positively, for which I express immense appreciation,

Such churches include Broadwater Baptist Church, Worthing, Portslade and Holland Road Baptist Churches (Brighton and Hove) and Peacehaven Evangelical Free Church. My contact with such fellowships evolved from either musical involvement there or through family and friends.

Involvement with Broadwater Baptist Church (BBC) arose through playing the organ for some years in the late 1990s, after a friend gave my name to the minister at the time, with whom I had a strong rapport and gained much blessing from his ministry and the fellowship.

My participation with Portslade and Holland Road Baptist churches originated through a close friend who was involved with both churches, which have strong connections with each other. I was warmly welcomed at those fellowships, where I attended afternoon meetings, my involvement coming about during my period of mental health issues, so was unable to continue my employment at Woodvale Crematorium. I will always be extremely grateful for the prayer support and encouragement of the ministers and members of those fellowships and groups over the years in which I was involved with them.

My connection with the church at Peacehaven was through a close pastor friend of Hugh and myself who often preached there throughout an extremely long interregnum. Hugh and myself visited there periodically and were significantly blessed by the welcome of the fellowship, worship and our friend's excellent preaching ministry.

In addition to being enormously blessed by my involvement with many fellowships, I have always been greatly encouraged by monthly one-to-one Bible Study and prayer meetings with close friends in Lancing over many years, and membership of 'Aglow', which offers strong fellowship, powerful worship and teaching (see chapter twelve).

I joined Aglow in 2013 through the lady who introduced me to the churches at Portslade and Holland Road. This dear friend has had a considerable positive impact upon me and kept me quite busy in my Christian journey since my early fifties - Including writing this book.

There are so many people through whom the Lord has blessed me in my life, and as I have written this chapter, I have thankfully brought to mind everybody to whom I have referred through this chapter and, indeed, this entire book.

The names of some close friends are included in my acknowledgements page at the start of my autobiography. I would love to be able to individually name everybody who has positively impacted my life, but it would be practically impossible. However, I remember everybody who has done so, and am incredibly thankful.

On my first visit to Lancing Tab in 1992, the first person to greet me was Ray Butler, one of the elders in that generation, who went to be with the Lord in 2014. Whilst not an ordained minister, Ray was a wonderfully gifted leader and speaker with an extremely large pastoral heart, whose custom was to address his congregations and audiences as "Loved Ones", thus telling them that they were dearly loved by the Lord Jesus,

Because I know that many people to whom I have referred knew/know the Lord, I feel that I can reliably refer to all special people in my life in both senses of the term, since the Lord loves all humanity whether or not they know His love and acknowledge Him as their personal Saviour.

Whilst many family members, friends and contacts for whom I have expressed appreciation are no longer alive, their positive impact and memory will always live on in my heart.

This chapter of appreciation is ultimately dedicated to the Lord, because it is ultimately by God's grace that I have been so abundantly protected, and through His Holy Spirit's presence and guidance that, despite life's challenges and storms, my life has been one of fulfilment and blessing.

I am sure that many people will be familiar with the chorus 'Count your blessings':

"Count your blessings, name them one by one, Count your blessings, see what God hath done:

Count your blessings, name them one by one; and it will surprise what the Lord hath done."

(Johnson Oatman Jnr)

Whilst an extremely old chorus, its truth does not age!

I close this chapter with the lyrics of a song which, whilst very short, summarises my view of and gratitude for my life. The text forms part of a thanksgiving poem entitled 'Gratefulness' which was written by George Herbert (1593–1633) and has touched my heart for many years:

Thou that hast given so much to me, give one thing more – a grateful heart.

Not thankful when it pleaseth me, as if thy blessings had spare days. But such a heart whose pulse may be thy praise.

Thou that hast given so much to me, give one thing more – a grateful heart."

CHAPTER ELEVEN
HEALING THROUGH DISCOVERY AND UNDERSTANDING

Call to me and I will answer you and tell you great and unsearchable
things you do not know.
(Jeremiah Ch.33v3)

Life can only be understood backwards, but it must be lived forwards.
Through experiences in recent years, I can strongly testify to the truth
found within the above quote by the Danish philosopher,
Soren Aabye Kierkegaard. (1813–1855)

Between 2014 and 2016, the Lord helped me to discover origins of
difficult issues which I experienced for much of my life. Such origins
were medical reasons which accounted for considerable emotional instability
and immature behaviour that I experienced and exhibited, although not
acknowledged in my early life.

My emotional fragility from early childhood was combined with a very
quick temper, both issues of which greatly exacerbated my difficulty in
expressing problems without breaking down. In early junior school, boys
in my class created the mantra of 'Temper, temper, Katherine Semper!'.
Although I recall the rhyme with much amusement nowadays, I obviously
did not find it funny at the age of seven, and inevitably, the crosser and more
worked up I became, the more they chanted it!

Whilst overcoming outbursts of temper as I grew older (outside my home
at least!), my ability to raise concerns without becoming emotional never
significantly abated even into adulthood. Well aware of my problem, I
attempted to mentally ignore or play down challenging situations in order to
avoid breaking down in front of people. However, that ploy only succeeded
for a limited period until I was confronted by 'the straw that broke the camel's
back', which caused my floodgates to open.

My parents and myself put the blame for excessive emotional issues
on throwbacks of frustration at not being understood, taunting and
in due course, natural feminine issues such as puberty and menstruation,
which exacerbated effects of personal issues. Whilst displaying excessive
emotion in adulthood was obviously abnormal in adulthood, I received
a reasonable amount of support, but with mental health issues not being

widely accepted or understood until more recent generations, pinpointing definite reasons for my frequent emotional outbursts was very difficult for people with whom I associated at school and work respectively.

When I sought employment at a job centre, a staff member recommended that I register as disabled, which would provide official   proof that my delays in seeking career training or employment were caused by genuine health issues such as my facial reconstructive surgery. After serious consideration I duly applied. The process involved completion of paperwork and an assessment with an independent doctor, who proved to be extremely supportive and sanctioned my registration. Being in the early 1980s, the criteria for being disabled was ambiguous, and usually limited to obvious physical conditions, such as immobility, blindness, etc. In recent generations, however, invisible mental and emotional conditions including Autism Spectrum Disorder (ASD) have also become recognised and accepted as disabilities.

My registration proved advantageous when applying for employment because, assuming that my qualifications, ability and experience were suitable, employers could fulfil their legal duty of employing somebody who was disabled without the need for practical adaptations in the workplace. However, with no recognised connections between physical and mental health conditions, appreciating reasons for my emotional upsets was understandably difficult for my managers and colleagues.

Unaware of such connections and ASD, as my life progressed I explored many avenues in my attempts to overcome my emotional demons, including counselling and prayer ministry. Whilst achieving degrees of improvement I never felt totally safe or peaceful. I would progress to longer periods without major incidents, only to be thrown by unexpected situations and fall back to square one. I always felt that I had a twofold problem, because in addition to difficult issues themselves, I felt very guilty and embarrassed about being upset. Whilst feminine issues did not help me, I could not hold them entirely responsible, having struggled emotionally all my life!

My long-term emotional healing began whilst I was working at Woodvale Crematorium when I was in my mid-fifties. Between 2014 and 2016 I suffered what amounted to a hormonal breakdown through a combination of a traumatic family bereavement, Congenital Hypothyroidsm (CH) and the menopause.

However, whilst that period of my life was extremely difficult and resulted in my retirement from Woodvale, I gained much knowledge and insight regarding my CH and received much love, care and support from family, friends, church, colleagues and medical professionals.

I received much support through prayer ministry regarding issues which I share within this chapter. I received some insights and revelations from totally unexpected sources, proving that the Lord's hand was in all the support which I received and confirmed Paul's proclamation in Romans Ch.8v28:

"And we know that in all things God works for the good of those who love Him, who have been called according to His purpose."

The chief discoveries which played substantial roles in my healing were my discovery that I had been affected by ASD for virtually all of my life, and also that my autism was compounded by anxiety and depression; all of which could almost certainly be linked to CH.

In chapter nine I shared the positive impact which my participation with Woodvale Crematorium and working relationships with many personnel there had upon my life.

When I became ill, it was largely advice and support from my manager and supervisor at Woodvale which helped me realise that the source of my long-term emotional problems was related to CH and ASD, although the connection had never been medically acknowledged.

Through a family member and family of college friends being affected by ASD, I learned much respecting both positive and challenging traits of autism.

Typical positive traits of people affected by ASD include possessing incredible levels of knowledge in their areas of ability and interest to the point of obsession. Upon understanding such traits I used to joke to family and people who knew me best that if I was autistic my 'specialist things' would be an encyclopaedic memory for dates (significant life occasions such as birthdays etc.), telephone and hymn numbers. Also, I was frequently the first Woodvale staff member to be approached about CD track numbers prior to the installation of the crematorium's computerised music system.

Nevertheless, despite my possession of such a trait, it had never occurred to me that I could be autistic because I led an active life, was sociable and could form strong and lasting friendships, especially with my increased self-confidence following my reconstructive facial surgery.

However, during a conversation with my manager at Woodvale, issues arose respecting both positive and negative traits of ASD, such as my memory and my problems when faced with unpredictable events. After our meeting, I experienced an 'Epiphany moment'. In my head I heard a gong and the words 'Amazing memory, problems with unexpected situations –- I could be autistic!'.

I learned that middle-aged people could be diagnosed with ASD, and on consideration of the strong possibility that I was autistic, I confided in my brother and sister-in-law and college friend. With our niece, and two members of my friend's family and husband being affected by ASD, they could quickly recognise ASD traits in other people and admitted that they had observed them in myself. Having experienced such insights, I requested my GP for a referral for an assessment for autism, and in due course received an appointment with a psychiatrist who was a specialist in ASD. In consequence of the two appointments which I attended and the consultant's evaluation of my completed ASD questionnaires, I learned that whilst not severely affected by ASD, I possessed a specific number of traits of High functioning Autism. This diagnosis was formerly known as Asperger Syndrome but within the past ten years, Asperger Syndrome has been placed under the general classification of ASD and is now officially referred to as High-functioning Autism

In retrospect, I learned that other characteristics which I had exhibited throughout my life, such as not concentrating when spoken to, not always reading social situations clearly, gullibility/naivety and lack of eye contact when addressing people are also typical traits of autism. However, with the condition not known about in the generation of my childhood and adolescence, such traits were seen as personality faults or manifestations of my lack of self-confidence.

However, when I discussed my diagnosis with my friend, she told me that, not only had she thought that I had ASD for a long time, but that she also strongly suspected that my father was affected, having met my parents a few times. I was amazed by this, but upon considering my friend's observations regarding my father, I reached the conclusion that she was perfectly correct.

With ASD not acknowledged until the 1990s when I was in my thirties, it was obviously never known about in my father's generation. Nevertheless, when I both recalled some remarks which my father had made during his life and contemplated what my friend had said about him, I later ascertained that my paternal grandfather also possessed traits of ASD.

Therefore, even though I believe that my autism was definitely connected to CH, alongside anxiety and depression, I doubtlessly also inherited from my paternal family.

Overall, my father had a very direct approach to life and, originating from northern England, he had a tendency to be somewhat outspoken: "Frank by name and Frank by nature" was my mother's wry comment when my father spoke or addressed issues in a less than diplomatic manner! Being quite a private and sensitive man overall, my father did not usually wear his heart on his sleeve, but, despite his intelligence, qualifications, practical skills, gifts and achievements, I recall him telling me and implying that he considered himself a failure in his life if he compared himself to his father.

Whilst some of my father's attitudes were both difficult and unfortunate, he never intended to hurt anybody, least of all my mother or myself, to whom he was totally devoted, and for whom he worked exceedingly hard in order to provide a secure and happy home and stable upbringing for me. When living with my parents in adulthood, I remember several occasions when my father was visibly very upset, because he genuinely could not understand why his actions or words had misfired, even though he would listen to explanations and endeavour to analyse respective scenarios.

During the final few months of my father's life, he became quite reflective, opening up at times and sharing poignant memories, some of which concerned hurts which had been caused by unfortunate attitudes of his father. My dear father had clearly buried these hurts throughout his entire life, hence the reason why he quite often considered himself to be a failure.

My mother and myself were considerably moved by what my father shared, neither of us requiring Einstein in order to understand the original source of my father's challenging personality traits at times.

However, finally learning about and understanding such origins helped me to virtually totally eradicate memories of difficult and hurtful situations involving my father. I also fully understood why my father was so anxious for me to be the best that I could be in my life; namely, so that I could potentially avoid feelings of failure which he experienced in his own life.

My father and myself had several heart-to-heart chats in the last months of his life, which I recall with great poignancy and affection. Those occasions were very special and resulted in a significant deepening of our relationship, enabling me to help him practically when necessary. Having always assumed the role of breadwinner and protector for my mother and myself, I think that privately, my father felt challenged in admitting that he needed physical and practical help at times, but outwardly he requested any needs and accepted help with dignity and gratitude.

With a combination of endorsing my friend's assertion that my father had been affected with ASD, and remembrance of what my father himself shared in his latter days, I developed an ongoing relationship of renewed love and depth with my father, albeit it one of memory rather than physical presence since he had gone to be with the Lord nearly ten years before I experienced the events and made the discoveries which form the foundation of this chapter.

In addition to my discoveries regarding ASD in the course of trying to help myself, I was amazed by what I learned about connections between CH and mental issues.

When I first experienced symptoms of significant emotional illness in my mid-fifties, I assumed – as did family friends and colleagues – that my problems were connected with the menopause. I received advice and support, and also read relevant medical literature and magazine articles in order to try to help myself.

In the course of my research, I was incredulous as to the number of references which were made to the thyroid gland and potential effects of relevant deficiencies and defects.

One magazine article exclusively relating to the thyroid gland was subtitled 'The forgotten organ' and highlighted the physical, mental and emotional impacts which an absent or malfunctioning thyroid gland can cause. Several articles which I read were written by international members of the medical profession, such authors commenting that thyroid-related problems were prone to being understated in the United Kingdom. Reading such literature provided my first ever awareness about the connections between CH and mental issues such as anxiety and depression.

I also read magazine articles written by people who suffered serious thyroid-related conditions including cancer, which resulted in their thyroid glands needing to be removed. The people described the significant impacts on their lives, such as the need to take daily medication for the rest of their lives, fatigue, anxiety and depression. Hypothyroidism is not uncommon as people age and medication will remedy the deficiency, but the issues to which I refer particularly relate to the absence of the gland, which I discovered is highly likely to have adverse impacts upon mental/emotional health as well as providing the necessity for regular medication in order to maintain physical health.

Reading such literature was both poignant and enlightening, as I came to realise that, whilst hitherto unknown to me, there had always been a valid reason for my lifelong problem with emotional instability, namely genuine anxiety/depression which could be directly linked to CH.

Through prayer ministry I was recommended to consider contacting Dr Brian McDonogh, whom I was told might well be able to help me respecting my CH-related issues. I duly contacted the doctor and made an appointment for an assessment consultation.

Dr McDonogh is a retired GP who set up a private practice including specialist branches of medicine such as Nutrition and Functional Medicine.

Functional medicine concerns the consideration of how the human body works together as a unit, and how the malfunction of one system of the body (cardio/respiratory, hormonal, etc.) can adversely affect systems of the body other than itself.

In Dr McDonogh, I discovered an amazing medical professional. I firmly believe that my first initial appointment was a real lifesaver, in which Dr McDonogh both confirmed many of my discoveries regarding my health concerns, and also told me relevant information which I had never known. Such knowledge greatly encouraged me and greatly assisted my psychological healing. I was recommended to obtain a number of supplements which would help me, but Dr McDonogh also emphatically stressed how I could help myself by long-term adoption and maintenance of healthy living regimes regarding diet, regular exercise, etc. As a Christian, Dr McDonogh included spiritual perspectives in his advice regarding healthy living, and is the first doctor to quote Scripture and songs in written summaries of my appointments!

The combination of such counsel could be summed up in the serenity prayer: "Lord, help me to accept the things I cannot change, courage to change the things I can and wisdom to know the difference."

The Lord has constantly blessed and challenged me through Dr McDonogh whom I continue to visit periodically, and himself, his wife and daughter have become personal friends of Hugh and myself.

Another revelation which I received when I was in my forties was that my need to wear glasses since the age of three was due to being long-sighted as a side effect of having been born with an abnormally small upper face rather than an optical defect. I cannot recall how the subject arose, but, during a routine optician appointment, I learned that all babies are long-sighted when they are born, but as their faces grow, their eyes normally correct themselves naturally. However, because my upper face was so small, due to a combination of my cleft palate and inherited family features, my eyes had no room in which to adjust, although I have always been told that they are extremely healthy to date.

My parents (especially my mother), were upset that I had to wear glasses, thinking that I had 'yet another' health problem, but having learnt the reason for being long-sighted, I have always felt pleased that the issue was due to one of my congenital medical conditions rather than a separate eye problem.

I never attempted to wear contact lenses, because having witnessed problems experienced by people who lost or dropped them, I do not feel that

I would manage the potential stress well! I am very happy wearing   glasses, especially with the vast choice of complementary frames which are available nowadays.

Although I reached middle-age before discovering answers to unresolved issues regarding my life, I can now testify to the blessings of freedom in my heart, which I sought for so many years.

Discoveries which I made about my CH-related psychological issues obviously did not practically obliterate such problems which I experienced in earlier life, but realising that emotional fragility was a definite by-product of CH has contributed enormously towards healing of painful memories and, especially, guilt and embarrassment which my upsets caused me, particularly during adulthood.

With my father's death in 2005 and my mother's development of vascular dementia from 2016, neither of my parents knew of my discoveries and healing which I share in this chapter. Regarding this reality, I feel a mixture of emotions.

I feel a sense of relief because my parents would have been mortified that they never knew that my psychological issues resulted from genuine sources such as CH and ASD, so expressed impatience or exasperation when I had emotional meltdowns over comparatively minor issues. However I also experience interwoven feelings of sadness and positivity, because whilst I am very sorry that I cannot share my recent discoveries with them, I know for certain that they would have been extremely proud and happy if I had been able do so and would have rejoiced in seeing how my experiences led to the emotional healing which I now know.

Through the prophet Joel, the Lord proclaimed:

"I will repay you for the years the locusts have eaten… You will have plenty to eat until you are full, and you will praise the name of the Lord your God, who has worked wonders for you…" (Joel Ch.2 vv25-26)

There is no cure for ASD, but knowing that I am autistic means that I can be aware of triggers and potentially difficult situations which I might encounter, so that I can reschedule plans or actions.

Nowadays I am much more confident about being able to raise issues of concern without becoming emotional, so problems do not escalate, and can also take myself less seriously and not see errors that I make as being the end of the world.

Although I inevitably do miss warning signs of triggers and, therefore experience emotional setbacks, such occasions are now definitely in the minority.

Consequently I am (largely!) far calmer and confident regarding my life, both inwardly and externally, a fact which has been observed by Hugh, close family and friends, about which I am extremely gratified.

Whilst I do not use CH-related issues or autism as a crutch, because I now know that I have an underlying reason for any 'hiccups', I cope with and 'get over' problems which I encounter comparatively quickly, and rarely feel overwhelmed with guilt and embarrassment for hours afterwards.

Prior to my above-mentioned discoveries, mindful of the fact that I was prone to emotional weakness, I viewed new chapters in life, such as courses or employment as fresh starts, and resolved not to become overwhelmed by problems. However, when incidents inevitably occurred, my demons caught up with me because, unaware of their origins, I was not prepared to deal with them.

Since my experiences of healing, I have shared the source of emotional issues with friends and former colleagues with whom I remain in contact, and I have received a number of extremely positive responses.

With there being widespread knowledge of conditions such as ASD in recent generations, I suspect that people who remembered me in connection with emotional upsets might have guessed that I had ASD, even if they did not realise that I had mental issues which were linked with a physical medical condition.

Had CH-related mental problems and ASD been recognised during my childhood/adolescence, my parents and myself would have received understanding and support from medical and education professionals, as well as family and friends who were aware of the sources of my emotional issues.

However, I doubt that my life would have been as fulfilled as it has been without knowing what I have in recent years, because I believe that my parents and myself might have been advised about possible limitations respecting education and employment. I also think that I might have been advised against certain activities, especially driving, because coordination can be a definite problem if affected by ASD. I might also have missed many leisure and music activities, courses and holidays in which I participated as I might never have had the confidence to go away on my own. In the event, unaware of being autistic and the fact that most of my psychological issues were by-products of my CH, whilst I struggled in some spheres of life, I have been blessed with a fulfilled life to date from perspectives of profession, relationships, leisure pursuits and disciplines – including passing my driving test after much stress.

Whilst being strong-willed has doubtlessly been exasperating for my loved ones at times, I believe that the characteristic was a gift from God, which gave me the strength to persevere in the life which He planned for me despite my medical conditions and challenges.

Amongst many biblical passages to which I can testify, two are found in

Isaiah's prophecy:

"So do not fear, for I am with you; do not be dismayed for I am your God. I will strengthen you and help you; I will uphold you with my righteous right hand." (Isaiah Ch. 41v10)

"Do not fear for I have redeemed you; I have summoned you by name; you are mine. When you pass through the waters, I will be with you; and when you pass through the rivers they will not sweep over you. When you walk through the fire, you will not be burned; the flames will not set you ablaze. For I am the Lord your God. The Holy One of Israel, your Saviour...." (Isaiah Ch.43 vv1b-3b)

Psalm 139 vv 13-16 which are quoted at the start of chapter five and chapter six these verses confirmed what I had learned who I am.

In January 2016 the Lord clearly spoke to me through a speaker at Aglow (see chapter twelve).

The message which I received was very enlightening, particularly following my discoveries and revelations in respect of my conditions. Especially importantly, the Lord's words strongly encouraged me to consider afresh the fact that I was made in the Lord's image and it was no mistake or inconvenience that I had been created in that way. The message referred to 'positive' ASD traits, which the Lord enables me to use for His glory. One such trait mentioned was that of my memory, since it enables me to remember important prayer requests, situations and people in specific need of prayer.

Since receiving that message from the Lord, in the most part I have been able to accept and value myself far more in the light of the passage from Psalm 139vv 13-16, since the verses confirmed what I had learned who I am and why I am as I am – from earthly and especially spiritual perspectives. Whilst the Lord longs for His children to continually grow in him, He knows, He accepts, loves and honours us where we are at in every stage of our lives.

It took me until middle age to reach the stage of fully understanding how the Lord sees me, although I still experience times of uncertainty, upon which the enemy will act in his attempts to sabotage my identity in the Lord and my efforts for Him. However, although he wins battles, the Lord will win the war.

As the Lord proclaimed through Jeremiah in his prophecy:

"I have loved you with an everlasting love; I have drawn you with unfailing kindness." (Ch31 v3) and

"Call to me and I will answer you and tell you great and unsearchable things you do not know." (Ch.33v3.)

Author R. J. Palacio wrote a novel entitled *Wonder* about a young boy who was born with a substantial facial deformity. On the novel's front cover, there is a quotation which reads:

"You can't blend in when you were born to stand out."

Whilst a work of fiction, the novel – also made into a blockbusting film – relates the story of Auggie and how he copes with life in the light of his deformity and all forms of attitude of people who encounter him, but ultimately he proves himself to shine out for his character and achievements. As consequences of both my medical conditions and not sharing many usual interests of the youth such as pop music etc., I frequently experienced challenges in blending in with my contemporaries, but the Lord's hand was upon me, and, through strong parental encouragement to always do my best, as they always hoped, I was also able to stand out from the crowd for my strengths, gifts and, not least, for my Christian faith.

As Christians we are called to stand out from the world, to be in it but not of it, as Jesus states in John's Gospel Ch.15 19 so we inevitably experience misunderstanding and ridicule.

In Paul's letter to the Romans Ch.1v16a, we read his declaration:

"For I am not ashamed of the gospel, because it is the power of God that brings salvation to everyone who believes…"

I am in possession of a Christian T-shirt which bears the words 'The Lord does not make mistakes! I'm meant to look like this!'. Whilst I am quite cautious as to when I wear it, I am generally not afraid to wear it, as, thanks to healing I received through the skills of the medical profession, I can honestly affirm that I am comfortable in my own skin.

I can testify to what the Lord has said to and done for me through many amazing sources.

The Lord proclaimed, "I am the Lord who heals you." (Exodus Ch.15v26) And I believe that He has!

CHAPTER TWELVE
WALKING WITH THE LORD

I will never leave you nor forsake you... Jesus Christ is the same yesterday,
today and forever.
(Hebrews Ch.13 v5&v8)

Since the world's creation, praise and thanksgiving have been offered to the
Lord, through Scripture, art, literature, music and believers' testimonies.

Having referred to my Christian faith throughout my autobiography, in
this chapter I share highlights of my testimony.

I was brought up in a Christian family, immediate family being members
of the Church of England, Methodist, Assemblies of God and Baptist
churches.

On marrying and moving to Abbots Langley, my parents attended Abbots
Langley Baptist Church (ALBC), so I consequently attended all children's
and youth events until I joined the choir of St Paul's Church, Langleybury
(StPL) when I was thirteen.

Once I became a chorister my parents gradually began to attend there
also. In due course, my mother was confirmed there and became fully
involved in church life until advancing years and the onset of vascular
dementia resulted in her moving to a Christian care home in Worthing in
2016. Whilst my father regularly worshipped at StPL until prevented by
failing health, he was not confirmed, having always been a strong member
of the Methodist Church.

Whilst no immediate family possessed a Catholic background, as
previously stated, my mother taught in the Abbots Langley RC primary
school for many years, and through my assisting her there from the musical
perspective on many occasions, I became familiar with Roman Catholic
worship.

Therefore, from childhood, I gained significant appreciation of most
Christian worship traditions, from the most to the least formal, all of
which have served in enhancing my personal faith. Such experience was also
advantageous from the professional perspective as an organist (see chapters
eight and nine).

Whilst I believed in God from very early memory and possessed a faith
from when I was about seven, I became a Christian in my early teens, and

was confirmed at StPL on 17 November 1974. My confirmation day was very special, and I remember the depth with which I made my statements of faith. However, whilst that day was and will always remain extremely important to me, in 1977 I felt led to make a further dedication of my life to the Lord, whilst on holiday in Ventnor, IOW, following a United Beach Mission meeting.

Church involvement being a normal part of my life from my earliest memory, it was rather ironic that my first experience of a church organ occurred in a hospital chapel, since ALBC did not possess an organ.

When I first joined StPL church choir, all services were those of traditional Church of England, i.e. Matins and Evensong, with extra services at the major festivals of Christmas and Easter. However, with progression of time and the advent of contemporary worship, Parish Communion and family services became regular forms of worship in addition to that of the traditional Book of Common Prayer.

My love of the 'English Choral Tradition' was born and greatly encouraged at StPL. Our choir periodically joined with other local church choirs in order to sing choral evensongs, cantatas and oratorios, both in a large church in Hemel Hempstead and St Albans Abbey/Cathedral.

StPL was affiliated to the Royal School of Church Music (RSCM), an organisation founded by Sir Sydney Nicholson in 1927 to promote high standards in all aspects of Christian worship. The RSCM holds many courses, events and summer schools throughout the UK, internationally and globally for corporate groups and individuals who are closely involved in church music.

Since playing the organ and being closely involved in Christian music, I have been a personal member of the RSCM and similar foundations. Through attending courses and events which were run by such organisations, I gained much musical and spiritual experience, encouragement and fellowship from course leaders and participants alike. All course directors and leaders were renowned in the world of church music, such as cathedral and collegiate church and chapel organists and directors of music. Many courses which I attended involved singing services in cathedrals and chapels, and it was extremely inspiring to associate with like-minded people, the majority of whom I believe were committed Christians.

Whilst foundations such as the RSCM used to almost exclusively concentrate upon traditional church music genres, in recent generations they have accommodated contemporary Christian music and worship styles, choirs and music ensembles in addition to traditional worship.

Being a member of an evangelical church and organisations as I am nowadays, the majority of the music which we sing in worship is of the contemporary genre, but I still greatly appreciate the beauty of traditional worship, such as hymns and anthems, etc., with my choice of Christian music to which I listen at home including an equal mixture of traditional and contemporary worship.

I definitely owe much of my knowledge and memory of Scripture to texts of all genres of Christian music which I have heard, sung and played.

Unfortunately, music and worship can cause significant division within churches and fellowships if believers do not respect traditions other than their own. Such controversy is dishonouring to the Lord, for whose praise and glory it is ultimately intended, as stated in the Westminster Confession of Faith:

"The chief end of man is to glorify God and enjoy Him forever."

All Christian music holds significant value, so it is vital not to throw out the baby with the bath water!

The well-known Victorian Baptist minister Charles Haddon Spurgeon (1834–1892) reputedly described the music as the war zone of the church in his generation. I wonder what he would have thought today!

Whilst music and worship has always been and is an extremely significant avenue of my Christian life and service, I would not be involved in such a field if my personal faith was not at its centre. Knowing that I believed all in which I participated considerably deepened my faith, even in my early years of involvement in Christian music at StPL when Church of England was as traditional as it came!

I have always been inspired by the depth and sincerity of the RSCM Choristers' prayer, which I quote in traditional language (although I believe there might/should be a version with contemporary language).

"Bless, O Lord, us Thy servants who minister in Thy temple. Grant that what we sing with our lips we may believe in our hearts, and what we believe in our hearts we may show forth in our lives, through Jesus Christ, Our Lord. Amen."

Irrespective of my varied avenues of involvement during my Christian journey, acknowledgement of faith in Jesus Christ as my personal Saviour has always been/will always be my ultimate priority.

A relative once asked me if I only/principally attended church from the musical perspective. Whilst pleased to honestly respond that my faith was central to my involvement at church, my relatives question was very thought-provoking, and I greatly admired him for asking it.

When a member at StPL, I appreciated the early morning communion services on Sundays, because they provided the opportunity for exclusive concentration on private worship and prayer.

During my final undergraduate year at Colchester, a combination of my studies and my participation in the college Christian Union and friends' church home group in my final year resulted in a great deepening of my faith. Throughout my student years at CISM, I increasingly realised that Colchester was definitely part of the Lord's plan for my life. As mentioned in chapter eight, in 1982 I was offered a place on a diploma course at the London College of Music, potentially following in my parents footsteps; but had to decline the place for financial reasons.

However, when I was accepted on the degree course at CISM I saw my acceptance on the course at LCM as an encouragement that I would undertake a professional music course one day but not at LCM because the Lord had a better course of action lined up for me - namely Colchester complete with the Christian music option.

Having been confirmed and rededicated my life to the Lord, I thought that I would have no further chance to openly witness what the Lord had done in my life since then. However, during a service at Elstree in which infant baptism (christenings) took place, I felt a call in my heart encouraging me to take the step of being baptised by believers' baptism.

One Sunday shortly before finishing college, I was travelling to Colchester by train. I sensed an urgency to alight at Ingatestone in order to attend the evening service at the Elim Pentecostal church, where our Christian Music Option group had visited. Whilst I did not know why, I just felt desperate to attend and have a chat with the pastor afterwards, although I had no idea what I wanted to say to him!

I was warmly greeted by Pastor Ian Moore and members of the congregation who remembered our group's visit. I clearly felt the Lord's presence throughout the service, and when the pastor proceeded to preach about believers' baptism, I realised that it was definitely the Lord who had guided me to attend that service, although I only felt led to alight at Ingatestone after the train had actually left Liverpool Street.

In the course of the sermon, the pastor effectively stated that there was no stipulation respecting timing of believers' calls to baptism, whether immediately, very soon or even years following conversion, because all circumstances and testimonies were unique to individual believers. I could not believe what I was hearing, because all that the pastor said fitted exactly how I had felt spiritually for quite some time.

Whilst I thought that the pastor could not have known that I would visit the church that evening, it later occurred to me that he might have received a word of knowledge (as described in 1 Corinthians Ch.12vv4-8 respecting the Spiritual gifts) so changed his sermon. I will never know for certain. All I recognised was that the Holy Spirit was definitely working in my heart that day. I was really excited and felt as if my eyes had come out like organ stops, to use a relevant synonym! The music student who was a member at Ingatestone was sitting next to me and later told me that I looked as if I had been totally 'zapped'!

The final song of the service was, "Be still for the presence of the Lord is moving in this place." With all the verses beginning with the words "Be still for the presence/glory/power of the Lord is moving in this place", the song confirmed my call to baptism, as if I needed further convincing. After the service, I met the pastor, obviously now knowing exactly what I wished to share with him! Having given a synopsis of my testimony and explained how I had felt led to attend at Ingatestone that evening, I requested to be baptised there and the pastor immediately and enthusiastically agreed. However, I was requested to tell the rector of my own church at Elstree that I wished to be baptised at Ingatestone, having attended there on occasion whilst a student at Colchester. The pastor offered to contact the rector himself if necessary, in order to assure him that he was not enticing me away from my membership there. Nevertheless, whilst my rector appreciated my telling him about wishing to be baptised, he had no problem with my decision.

I was baptised on 1st October 1989, after which the pastor shared his perspective of my impromptu attendance at the evening service in June, and especially, his observation of my close attention whilst he was preaching about baptism followed by my meeting with him in order to request to be baptised.

Whilst on a 'spiritual high' for the immediate period following my baptism, over the next few years my Christian life continued to primarily centre around my involvement in the traditional music and worship at Elstree, and where I also served on the church's council for several years.

However, as time progressed, as much as I appreciated the privilege of my role as Director of Music, and the friendship which I received from the rector, his wife and many church members, I missed regular midweek activities such as homegroups which incorporated Bible study and prayer meetings etc., which were somewhat lacking at Elstree.

In chapter eight I briefly shared how my postgraduate employment in the Watford DSS led to becoming involved with Christchurch Baptist (CCB), Kings Langley where I was originally dedicated. At my successful interview for reinstatement in the Civil Service, one of my interviewers and initial DSS manager was Paul Tucker, whom, as I sensed at my interview, was a committed Christian. Shortly after commencing work in the DSS, I learned that Paul and his wife were members at CCB, and, on enquiry, discovered that CCB hosted all the activities which I was seeking, in addition to regular Sunday evening worship, which had long since discontinued at Elstree.

I began to attend CCB and received an extremely warm welcome from

Rev. Graham Sparkes, the minister in that season, Paul, the church Lay Assistant and all the fellowship. I enjoyed increasing involvement at CCB and became a member in 1991.

CCB was the first non-Conformist church of which I was a member, and incorporated traditional and contemporary worship, led by an organist, choir and music group according to respective services and music genres. I participated in all aspects of the music and worship of the church, and, combined with homegroup and other activities, thoroughly enjoyed my years there until I moved to Lancing, following the marriage of Hugh and myself.

I made long-term friendships at CCB, including a number in my age range with whom I attended Spring Harvest on two occasions through which I gained great blessing. The first time was especially memorable and exciting since, due to circumstances, I joined the group at extremely short notice with the authority and blessing of Paul Tucker, my manager, since nobody else in my grade was on leave that week.

Having never attended a mass Christian event before, it was an amazing experience to spend nearly a week with several thousand Christians in addition to fellowship with our own parties, whether in the context of seminars and worship or enjoying the leisure facilities of the Butlins facilities at Pwllheli and Minehead, and times outside the campus.

When Hugh and myself began courting in 1992, we regularly visited each other's churches at Elstree, CCB and Lancing Tabernacle (the Tab), where our respective friends became friends of us both. We became engaged in 1993 and were married at CCB on 16 July 1994.

Graham Sparkes was on sabbatical when we married, so most of our marriage service was conducted by Paul Tucker, with the address being given by the late Rev. Max Donald, the pastor at Lancing Tab in the early 1990s. Also, with both Max and his wife, Ruth being extremely musically gifted, they performed one of Max's own compositions during the signing of the registers.

On moving to Lancing, I duly became a member at Lancing Tab, which has always had an extremely godly leadership team and been known as a strong and vibrant church within the community of Lancing. However, for personal reasons I spent a period of time in membership at Lancing Methodist Church (LMC), having played the organ there for monthly services, funerals and weddings as required since 1995. With Hugh, family and close friends all being involved at Lancing Tab, this was an extremely difficult decision to make, but in consequence of prayerful consideration and discussion with Hugh, I felt that the Lord was calling me to serve Him in

LMC for a season. Those years included the centenary year of LMC in 2004, thus involving special events and services. However, I maintained contact with Lancing Tab and continued to attend activities and services there. In addition to participation in the music, I also became involved in pastoral care at LMC, which was a new avenue of Christian service for me, which I found extremely rewarding.

From 2018, I felt that the Lord was leading me to return to membership at Lancing Tab. Initially attending evening services on a regular basis, I joined a pastoral group with Hugh and attended special morning services, once such occasion being the baptism of our niece, Sarah, which played an especially influential role in my return to Tab membership. Following prayerful consideration and discussion with Hugh, the leadership team and friends at the Tab, I was received into membership in April 2019, the year in which Hugh and myself celebrated our Silver Wedding anniversary.

Therefore, I was fully involved in Lancing Tab for the final year of John Woods' twenty-two years' pastorate, the ensuing interregnum, selection process and appointment of Barnaby Monteiro, the new pastor, most of which occurred virtually due to the coronavirus lockdown.

I had continued to play the organ for Sunday morning services at LMC and occasional services until the suspension of corporate worship due to Covid-19, but when lockdown restrictions eased, I joined the Tab musicians' team, so withdrew from most participation at LMC on Sundays.

In addition to musical participation and membership of our pastoral group, Hugh and I also joined the Tab's welcoming and pastoral visiting teams, such ministry being a great responsibility and privilege.

Whilst I feel immensely privileged to be involved in music in worship, I also experience significant blessing in fields of Christian service where music is not primarily or solely involved.

In addition to fields of activity and service with which Hugh and myself are involved at Lancing Tab, over a significant number of years I have been involved with Aglow, Living Hope Ministries and ministries which support persecuted believers throughout the world.

Commencing in 1967 through just four ladies praying, Aglow developed into a movement which has currently reached over one hundred and seventy nations; its motto being 'Every nation touched, Every heart changed'. Governed by national and international boards, Aglow's chief objective is to evangelise to and to pray for hitherto unreached parts of the world. Aglow members meet in geographical locations, with day and residential conferences being held nationally, internationally and globally. A highlight is the annual national weekend conference which is held in Southport. Originally an exclusively ladies organisation, in recent decades Aglow has welcomed men, with increasing number of men's groups being formed, which are known as 'Men of Issachar'.

Living Hope Ministries (LHM) began in 1994, when the Lord sowed a seed in the heart of a pastor in Lancing named Richard Brunton who is an elder at Lancing Tab.

The objective of LHM is to train church pastors and leaders in nations of the world which, due to personal circumstances such as finance, would never be able to attend formal Bible college. Such training enables those pastors and church leaders to minister to their own congregations and fellowships. LHM has blessed many individuals and corporate fellowships in many nations within the majority of our world's continents, through Pastor Brunton's initial obedience in following the Lord's calling.

There are three ministries which exclusively support persecuted Christians, both individually and corporately, namely Barnabus Fund, Release International and Open Doors, with which I have been predominantly involved, including appreciating the privilege of being a church representative since 2001.

I find it both incredibly amazing and sobering to consider the depth of faith which persecuted believers possess, and their willingness to endure any form of persecution. Such Christians refuse to relinquish their faith at any cost, including the ultimate risk of sacrificing their lives for the sake of the Gospel.

The 'Persecuted Church' can be/is also referred to as the 'Perseverance Church' due to its fellowships and individual believers stalwartly persevering in their faith despite opposition and suffering.

It is a known fact that much revival occurs within nations of the world where persecution is rife.

Whilst Covid-related prohibition of corporate worship was instigated for reasons of protection and safety, Christians who can normally worship freely experienced a taste of what it must be like never to be able to worship God corporately and share fellowship with Christian brothers and sisters. I think that such limitations have proved that formats of Christian worship are immaterial. The sole purpose of Christian worship is to praise God for who He is and His love for His world; most importantly, sending Jesus to earth to minister, suffer and die to pay the price for the world's sin, so that all who accept Him as their personal Saviour will enjoy eternal life with Him when earthly life ends.

Whilst unable to include details due to limitations of space, Hugh and myself also felt humbly privileged to sponsor several children in Africa and Asia through Christian organisations and charities, thus offering them educational, material and medical needs which we take for granted in the Western world.

I commenced this chapter by stating that, for practical reasons of space, I would be obliged to limit its contents to what I consider are the most influential parts of my Christian journey. However, creating even a short list of highlights has proved very challenging, such has been the diversity of my personal pilgrimage: influences of upbringing, encouragement of Christian family and friends, avenues of Christian worship/activity, and special events such as confirmation and baptism.

Whilst appreciating my Christian upbringing, I bear special testimony to the influence of my maternal grandparents, who were members of the Assemblies of God church in South Harrow, Middlesex.

When I stayed with my grandparents during childhood and adolescence, I enjoyed attending church with them, and remember being intrigued by their totally informal and spontaneous form of worship, and the midweek activities which they attended, such as Bible Studies and prayer meetings. Once involved in evangelical churches myself, where such worship and meetings were the norm, I felt a sense of joy that I was/am following in my grandparents' footsteps. As our church in Lancing pray for church members and their family members regarding special circumstances and needs, I realise how my grandparents' church would have prayed for me regarding medical issues, and rejoiced when my grandparents shared that I had become a Christian during my teens.

I found my first experience of Spring Harvest very poignant, because my grandparents attended equivalent events, and I wished that they had been alive then, so that we could have shared experiences.

My grandparents toured the Holy Land when I was very young, so when Hugh and I visited Israel I felt that it was a great privilege and blessing to be following their example.

Both of my maternal grandparents went to be with the Lord in 1980, after which I did not experience further regular contemporary or charismatic worship until I began my student days at Colchester.

As with negative attitudes respecting music and worship styles, considerable damage and divisions can too often be caused between believers who do or do not advocate charismatic worship and influence. I admit that I encountered some unfortunate/unfavourable attitudes, which implied a superior or inferior level of Christian faith, which I found somewhat concerning. However, I met many believers who expressed such loving and inviting personae, I felt that there was something 'different' about them, which was obviously the working of the Holy Spirit in their lives.

Although my grandparents were charismatic, unfortunately my faith and Christian experience were not of the maturity for me to discuss the subject with them whilst they were alive.

I thus sought to learn from friends who showed positive attitudes of possessing charismatic faith, since I desired to know the experience which they had, and hopefully to demonstrate the same qualities and attraction. Therefore, through discussion, Bible study and prayer I became a charismatic believer. Derived from the Greek word *Charisma* (a free gift of grace), charismatic is the term which is used within Scripture in order to describe a wide range of supernatural experiences. In particular, they include the spiritual gifts which are listed in 1 Corinthians Ch12-14.

According to the Bible, all Christians possess the Holy Spirit, and acknowledge His importance as the third person of the Trinity, i.e. Father, Son and Holy Spirit. Bible-believing Christians accept that their walk with God can continually deepen and develop, but the key factor in this process is the Holy Spirit. The Bible teaches that the manifestation of the Holy Spirit as seen in the first-century church (such as healing, miracles, prophecy, speaking in/interpretation of tongues, etc.), are available to contemporary believers and should be practised and experienced today.

I emphasise that being a charismatic believer does not make me a 'superior' Christian, and definitely does not mean that I will receive extra rewards from the Lord when I ultimately enter eternity.

On the contrary, since I profess my possession of the Lord's presence and blessings in a special way, the Lord requires me to witness to my faith and love for Him through evidently exercising the fruit of the Holy Spirit in my life. Such instruction is clearly stated within Scripture. In Galatians Ch.5vv22-23, Paul speaks of the fruit of the Holy Spirit including nine qualities, namely: love, joy, peace, forbearance, kindness, goodness, faithfulness, gentleness and self-control. The fact that 'fruit' is referred to in the singular implies that believers should demonstrate possession of all nine of the qualities, the concept of which is quite thought-provoking and challenging.

This teaching is in contrast with the gifts of the Holy Spirit as recorded in 1 Corinthians Ch.12 vv7-11, where Paul states believers can be expected to possess some gifts but not all of them.

However, Paul states that love is the most important quality to demonstrate, without which no service or action for the Lord or other people will be worthwhile or meaningful. (Paul's definition of love is agape' genuine selfless love, described in 1 Corinthians Ch.13.)

Whilst I have experience of spiritual gifts, including the Lord speaking to and guiding me powerfully, to date, I have not witnessed any miraculous healings from life-threatening/long-term illness or injury, although I have heard testimonies of such events from family, friends and church members. One such healing was experienced by my maternal grandmother, who suffered heart and chest conditions throughout her life. During comparatively early adulthood, she suffered one severe illness from which my grandfather and family were warned that she might not recover. However, my grandmother 'turned the corner' at the exact time that some members of the AOG prayed for her, having gathered specifically to do so and proceeded to make a full recovery from her ill-health on that occasion. Consequently, my grandparents became strongly involved in that church for the rest of their lives, fulfilling prominent roles such as the missionary secretary and treasurer for many years.

Although I did not experience instantaneous or dramatic healing from my medical conditions, the facts that I recovered from some surgery significantly more quickly than average according to the medical profession, and the Lord has honoured me by using me for His service, are testimonies to His faithfulness and healing love during my life.

In addition to my avenues of Christian service in which I have recognised the Lord's leading, I have also been greatly blessed through experiences such as personal Christian studies and visiting the Holy Land and biblical sites visited by Paul in the course of his ministry.

When choosing my O-level/CSE options at school, I was disappointed because, due to both music and religious education (RE) being in the 'specialist subject' option block I could not take RE because I was taking music. However, since living in Lancing I found Christian/Bible study courses which I thoroughly enjoyed pursuing, which led to achieving certificates authorised by comparatively obscure Bible societies and colleges, although the tutors were extremely scholarly and godly men. For one of my studies I wrote a thesis on 'Death and Resurrection'," in which I was able to incorporate much of my work and experience in the funeral and bereavement field. I have also always much appreciated one-to-one Bible-study which I have undertaken with close friends over many years in addition to studies in which I was involved at CCB, and Hugh and I have been involved at Lancing Tab and Tab related groups.

BIBLICAL TOURS

I have visited Israel twice with Glyn Morgan's holiday organisation (see chapter ten) in 1992 (prior to Hugh and myself beginning our courtship) then with Hugh in autumn 1998. As previously recorded, my maternal grandparents toured the Holy Land when I was very young, so when Hugh and I visited Israel, I felt privileged in realising that this was another dimension in which I was following in their footsteps.

Visiting biblical sites were amazing experiences which brought the Bible alive, both in Israel and on a Christian cruise in the Aegean Sea entitled 'In the steps of St Paul'. The latter holiday was organised by Maranatha Tours. 'Maranatha' is Aramaic, meaning 'The Lord is Coming' or 'Come, O Lord/Lord Jesus'.

Since participating in such tours, memories of well-known biblical sites have always held fresh meaning, especially those associated with key events of the Christian faith. Classic examples are those of Jesus' birth, death and resurrection, Pentecost, Paul's ministry within his many epistles and John's exile to Patmos, where he wrote the book of Revelation.

One major attraction of the Israel holidays led by Glyn Morgan was that, unlike many Holy Land tours, we stayed in just one resort for our entire holiday. Thus, whilst tour days were long, we were not living out of suitcases, so appreciated returning to our excellent hotel in Netanya for meals, meetings and relaxation each evening, and enjoying its facilities and those of Netanya itself when we were not on tours.

All the tours were extremely meaningful, with either Glyn Morgan or other ministry leaders reading relevant Scripture passages at each site, which were also the focus of our evening meetings.

Our Israel tours began by visiting Emmaus, where Jesus visited on the evening of His resurrection day, because Glyn Morgan, our leader, believed that Emmaus reminded us that we serve a living Saviour.

Whilst visiting all the biblical sites was special, specific experiences appreciated by Hugh and myself, both individually and jointly, included the Church of the Holy Nativity, Sea of Galilee – with its beautiful surrounding hills and scenery – and our boat trip on the lake in glorious weather, witnessing the baptism of some of our party in the River Jordan, Jerusalem, and the Garden Tomb.

Respecting the crucifixion, Scripture states that the crucifixion occurred at Golgotha, meaning 'The place of the skull', and when visiting the Garden Tomb, it was definitely possible to see the path which would have been taken on the final stage of the procession to the site of Jesus' crucifixion. The skull which was carved within the rock opposite the Garden Tomb was also extremely clear, thus making the experience of visiting the immediate vicinity of Christ's death extremely authentic.

Our party shared in a communion service within the Garden Tomb and viewed the tomb in which Jesus was laid, with its door bearing the immortal words spoken by the two angels recorded in the Gospel of Luke Ch.24v6: "He is risen!"

My first visit to Israel took place in early December, and on the final day I took advantage of a second visit to Bethlehem prior to our journey to Tel Aviv airport and our flight back to the United Kingdom.

Glyn Morgan led a brief act of worship at the reputed exact site of Jesus' birth in the Church of the Holy Nativity, the experience of which made Christmas 1992 feel extra special.

As the title suggested, the Aegean Sea cruise focused on Paul's ministry and teaching, with our site visits including Athens, Beroea Corinth, Ephesus, Patmos, Pergamum, Philippi and Thessalonica.

Both separately and jointly, Hugh and myself were especially impressed by Ephesus, Philippi and Patmos. It was really possible to imagine such locations in the generations that we read about in Scripture.

Participants on the cruise numbered in the hundreds, with many 52-seater coaches required to ferry everybody to the various sites whilst ashore. The procession must have looked amazing to pedestrians who saw them (although motorists were possibly not too happy with the number of coaches which they were required to travel between and behind!). Both on excursions and aboard the ship, the atmosphere and fellowship was extremely positive, since all participants were on the same mission.

As I approach the end of this chapter, I reiterate that the testimony which I have shared represent the examples of what the Lord has done in my life, which I regretfully have been unable to include. I testify to the Lord's hand being upon me through all the blessings and challenges of my life to date, and those which I will experience until I enter eternity, and am reunited with family, friends and Christian brothers and sisters who have preceded and will follow me there. It is a certain joy to know that one day every believer will experience an eternity where there will be nothing at all that is bad, as stated in Revelation Ch.21v4.

I close with the final lines of one of countless hymns written by Fanny Crosby (1920–1915)

"When my spirit, clothed immortal, wings its flight to realms of day, This my song through endless ages, Jesus led me all the way."

("All the way my Saviour leads me" v3)

CONCLUSION

I thank my God every time I remember you, In all my prayers for all of you, I always pray with joy, because of your partnership in the gospel from the first day until now, being confident of this, that He who began a good work in you will carry it on to completion until the day of Christ Jesus.

(Phil.Ch1vv3-6)

During the months that I have been writing my autobiography, I have experienced freedom through circumstances which occurred during that period, in addition to making the discovery that my writing has proved extremely cathartic for me.

A predominant conclusion which I have reached is that, overall, the negative challenges of my life have been strongly outweighed by the positive, and that I have so much to rejoice in and thank God for.

Extremely importantly, I feel that writing my story has challenged me to seriously consider all that I have written, so that my writing has effectively served as an ongoing renewed dedication to the Lord.

The Lord wants the best for His children, His 'best' being that we will all conform to the image of Christ, so that His perfect will might be fulfilled in our lives.

As I have written and constantly revised this book, I have experienced a significant level of understanding, and healing respecting challenges and difficulties (see chapter eleven).

My inclusion of painful circumstances and memories are definitely not intended as a pitiful rendition of 'My Life and Hard Times' (to quote the title of James Thurber's book), but simply as 'matters of fact' which occurred and affected my life from both positive and negative perspectives. A combination of my personal discoveries and a chapter in the bestselling Christian novel *The Shack** enabled me to consciously and prayerfully choose to fully forgive everybody whose attitudes towards me respecting my medical conditions and related issues were decidedly unsupportive and caused considerable hurt, whether through deliberate spite or unintentional lack of thoughtfulness and tact.

Exercising complete forgiveness is a challenging process, because there are times when current situations will inadvertently evoke memories of past deep-seated psychological hurt. However, in such circumstances, the answer is to prayerfully recall my choice to forgive and seek God's strength to do so.

Whilst I am in no way there yet, regarding exhibiting one hundred per cent forgiveness and forgetting past hurts, as the speaker and prolific authoress Joyce Meyer states:

"I am not where I want to be yet, but I am not where I was." In Paul's letter to the Philippians Ch.3, Paul wrote;

"...forgetting what is behind and straining towards what is ahead, I press on towards the goal to win the prize for which God has called me heavenward in Christ Jesus." (vv13b-14)

Whilst total forgiveness of people who inflict serious hurt on individuals can be extremely difficult, the ability to do so serves as a significant release for the injured party and can prevent serious physical and/ or psychological illness as a result of harbouring resentment and illness throughout life.

I can testify to the freedom which I have experienced through making the choice to forgive people who discriminated against and rejected me, particularly throughout my childhood and adolescence.

Perpetrators of harmful attitudes, words and actions may genuinely never be aware of the effects which their behaviour have on people, long-term, or know or care about being forgiven, but true forgiveness, such as I can choose to offer as a Christian, releases them into the Lord's care and control.

I quote the refrain of a contemporary version of the hymn 'Amazing Grace' which is very true for me, since it speaks of release from negative experiences in life.

"My chains are gone! I've been set free, My God my Saviour has ransomed me,

And like a flood, His mercy reigns, Unending love! Amazing Grace." (Chris Tomlin and Louie Giglou)

Both my title and subtitle for this book are inspired by two comments which I clearly remember. The title, 'God broke the mould' was influenced by part of a sermon preached by a pastor friend who was emphasising the uniqueness of every human being.

My subtitle, 'Nobody like me, Nobody like you' testifies to healing of a hurtful memory which I could never have contemplated using until comparatively recently, having been a definite taunt respecting my irregular facial appearance in my mid-teens. The remark, made by a school contemporary was effectively that I would never be mistaken for another person because there was nobody else who looked like me.

Nevertheless, whilst the remark was unfortunately deliberate, factually my peer was quite correct, because everybody is different, with even identical twins having different DNA. Thus, I felt that the Lord enabled me to recognise the pupil's comment as a positive remark, through which I can celebrate the fact that there *is* nobody else like me or anybody else, so I could use both comments to emphasise the fact in naming my book, alongside the cover design with many people of every size, shape and colour!

Previously quoted, I reiterate 1 Samuel Ch.16v7 which states that people look at the outward appearance of other people, but God looks at their hearts, and whatever he sees, God loves every human being equally and as dearly as if they were the only person on the planet.

I share the words of a lovely song which was introduced to me by a pastor and wife from whom I received prayer ministry some years ago.

"Show me, dear Lord, how you see me through your eyes, so that I may realise Your great love for me.

Teach me, O Lord, that I am precious in Your sight. As a Father loves His child, so You love me.

Refrain: I am Yours because You have chosen me, I'm Your child, because You've called my name,

And Your steadfast love will never change. I will always be Your precious child.

Show me, dear Lord, that I can never earn Your love, That a gift cannot be earned only given.

Teach me, O Lord, that Your love will never fade, that I can never drive away Your great love for me."

Refrain:

(Andy Park - "In the Secret" Vineyard Voices - 2004)

There are so many hurting people in the world today who sadly claim that they have never known genuine unconditional love or a sense of self-worth from anybody, so the concept of them appreciating God's love just as they are might be extremely difficult to appreciate. Thus, effective Christian witness is vitally important.

The British writer William J. Thoms (1803–1855) stated a very profound truth:

"Be careful how you live. You may be the only Bible that some person ever reads."

I also quote the profound truth which was stated by Dr Seuss:

"You may be one person to the world, but to one person you may be the world."

If a believer is 'the world to one person', they might be the one person who shares about the Lord.

As I have written about many people who have meant so much to me but are no longer alive, realisation respecting the progression of time and advancing of my own age has dawned upon me. This fact is especially true when I consider people I knew and loved who passed away in their fifties or sixties.

As a child, adolescent and young adult, whilst I knew that people who died before reaching their seventies had passed away comparatively young, the concept of reaching my own fifties and sixties seemed an extremely long way ahead!

However, having now reached my early sixties, the comprehension that I have now exceeded the age that a number of loved family members and friends reached is somewhat sobering to consider.

Psalm 90 v10 states that the allocation of years on earth is seventy or eighty if we are strong. The King James translation of 'seventy' is "three score years and ten", so by the latter description of age, I am obliged to acknowledge that I have competed the 'three score' years and am into the extra 'ten'!

With increasing numbers of people, certainly in the Western world, reaching their eighties, nineties and even centenaries in recent generations, reaching one's sixties seems ever younger, and I certainly do not feel old! Nevertheless, according to Scripture, eternity is considerably nearer than it was for me!

Whilst on this earth I continue to endeavour to live and enjoy as healthy and fulfilled a life as possible. In John Ch.10v10, having been referring to Himself as "Good Shepherd", Jesus states that He has come that His sheep (people) can know life in all its fullness.

However, whilst doing so I cannot deny the fact that I also greatly look forward to realising God's promises respecting an eternity with Him, which will be totally devoid of evil and suffering, as recorded in Revelation Ch.21vv1-7 particularly vv3-4:

"…And I heard a loud voice from the throne saying 'Look, Gods' dwelling place is now among the people and He will dwell with them. They will be His people, and God Himself will be with them and be their God. He will wipe away every tear from their eyes. There will be no more death, or mourning, or crying or pain, for the old order of things has passed away.'"

This text is a favourite Bible passage which I hope will be read at my thanksgiving service in due course.

With our world in its current state of turbulence, the promises speak of real encouragement for all Christians who know that one day they will dwell with Him for eternity. Additionally, having always been prone to being emotional throughout my life, the concept of no crying in eternity serves as a promise of real healing for me, although my homecall will probably result in a substantial drop in sales for manufacturers of handkerchiefs and tissues!

In addition to the experiences of healing which are included in my autobiography, I feel calmer as I consider the realisation that as I age, both the desperately sad state of our world and many challenging circumstances, especially those such as 'everyday practical frustrations' seem less important when I consider the prospect of a perfect eternity.

Paul states: "I consider that our present sufferings are not worth comparing with the glory that will be revealed in us." (Romans Ch.8v18)

In addition to the above passage from Revelation, I also hope that the following verses can be justifiably included in my eventual thanksgiving service:

"For I have been poured out like a drink offering, and the time for my departure is near. I have fought the good fight, I have finished the race, I have kept the faith. Now there is in store for me the crown of righteousness, which the Lord, the righteous judge, will award to me on that day, and not only to me, but also to all who have longed for His appearing." (2 Timothy Ch.4vv6-8)

The conclusion to this autobiography is followed by a bibliography and sources of reference for facts shared within this book and a list of contact details of foundations, organisations and charities to which I have referred.

I hope that my life story will have proved encouraging overall, empathetic if any readers have been able to relate to things which I have shared, either for themselves or people they know, and provided some amusement along the way.

I pray that the Lord will bless you. Katy Christopher.

March 2022

*The Shack, by Wm Paul Young. Ch.16 A Morning of Sorrows, esp pp224–225

pub Hodder Windblown Media

MEDICAL ADDENDUM

Whilst my autobiography includes all aspects of my life, due to the medical conditions with which I was born, it possesses a medical thread which is inevitably woven throughout the book. Due to Congenital Hypothyroidism necessitating lifelong medication/medical reviews, and my cleft palate entailing surgery and treatment from birth until early adulthood, involvement with the medical profession have been and will always be part of my life. Hence virtually all chapters of this book include medical references, with a few concentrating upon experiences which had specific positive impacts upon my life.

However, my life story is not intended to read as a medical treatise, and whilst I share some of my challenging experiences, I hope that readers will recognise that I am not doing so to relate a catalogue of doom and gloom, but in order to share the positive impact which my medical history had upon my life, not least regarding my career and Christian testimony.

Medical science has advanced incredibly throughout history and continues to do so on a huge scale. Obvious examples include pioneering life-saving surgery, treatment and drugs within all fields of medicine, and during my life I have learned of much research and many advances respecting the understanding and treatment of both CH and clefts from both physical and psychological perspectives.

Whilst I have personally benefitted from some such advances regarding my conditions, many results of medical research have helped/are helping children who were born in successive generations to myself.

Significant advances and developments respecting CH and clefts have included:

*The neonatal heel prick test, which screens for a number of serious health issues, including CH.

*Recognition of connections between CH and mental health issues, such as anxiety/depression and possibly also, Autism Spectrum Disorder (ASD) in addition to physical and intellectual disabilities if a diagnosis of CH is substantially delayed.

*Detection of clefts during the routine ultrasound scans at twenty weeks of pregnancy, so that preparations can be made for necessary support to be in place for the baby and family immediately upon birth. Such scans have detected cleft lips since the early 1980s, although the detection rate was originally as low as five per cent. However, nowadays with the great advancement of modern technology and improved training for medical technicians, about eighty per cent of cleft lips are detected at the twenty-week scan. 3D scans are also used which offer a clear view of the face, so are more effective in detecting cleft lips and also cleft palates, which are very difficult to detect in the routine scan. 3D scans are typically only offered through private care, although some cleft centres offer them to parents who receive a diagnosis of a cleft, and some private centres will also offer them for free, so parents can be prepared for what their baby will look like once born.

*The advent of reconstructive facial surgery in order to correct Midface Retrusion (distortion of facial growth), which is often experienced by patients born with clefts as they approach and reach adolescence.

*The foundation of the Cleft Lip and Palate Association.

*Substantially developed medical professional-parental relationships and much stronger support for parents and families of children who require hospital admission, especially on a regular or long-term basis.

*The foundation of charities which enable parents to stay with children in hospital and families to remain together in accommodation near hospitals, and support for patients' siblings such as their being able to attend hospital schools alongside patients themselves. Such support provides as much psychological support as physical treatment for patients, children and families.

Undoubtedly the medical development which specifically impacted my life was the surgery which became available in the 1970s in order to correct MR. When I was about nine, in my absence, my mother asked a GOSH orthodontist if there was any treatment which would enable my jaws and teeth to meet normally. In the late 1960s the answer was negative, but less than ten years later such a procedure was pioneered, which I underwent when I was eighteen, and upon which I have particularly focused in chapter seven.

Research has been undertaken since the last century respecting MR as a side-issue of cleft repair. In 1920, a significant medical report was written about the issue by Harold Gillies (a plastic surgeon) and Captain W. Kelsey Fry (a senior dental surgeon). The report suggested that MR was caused by the repair of cleft palates during infancy.

In the 1950s, the German 'Schweckendiek' technique recommended leaving the hard palate open until individuals' early teenage years. This approach was duly adopted by European cleft centres (albeit it with variations) although such papers carried less importance since they were unpublished. In 1959, a paper was published by Ortiz Monasterio, a Mexican plastic surgeon. Monasterio recorded nineteen patients who did not undergo palatal repair in infancy and good facial growth was reported. However, the clear disadvantage of this theory was that while facial growth was normal, the quality of individuals' speech was inevitably poor.

In 1982, Michael Mars, one of my GOSH consultants, felt a concern to research the assumption that cleft palate repair surgery which was performed in infancy was responsible for MR during adolescence. An opportunity arose for the examination and documentation of many people in Sri Lanka who were born with clefts, but for significant reasons, such as poverty, had never undergone repair surgery. In due course, over six hundred patients underwent repair surgery. Their results were recorded and followed up between 1984 and 2009 and, significantly, such people did not suffer MR afterwards.

Whilst the Sri Lankan Cleft Lip and Palate project began for reasons of research, it developed into a care programme, with multidisciplinary teams visiting Sri Lanka over a period of many years. Academically, a large number of qualifications and papers were achieved and published in consequence of the project/research.

Unfortunately, however, whilst research has clearly proved that MR is avoided if cleft repair surgery is avoided, in nations such as Sri Lanka, individuals affected by clefts stand to experience considerable stigmas, prejudice and ostracisation if their clefts cannot be repaired early in their lives. This is because unrepaired cleft lips result in abnormal facial appearance, and unrepaired cleft palates will cause the speech of people who are affected to be virtually unintelligible. Even after repair in later life, there are risks of continuing discrimination.

I think that it is true to state that, within the Western world, research and pioneering surgical techniques and treatment are virtually constantly ongoing, and techniques have now been developed which cause less deformity if initial cleft palate repair is performed during infancy.

There are still specialist cleft centres which claim that MR is unavoidable, but it is less of an issue now that corrective surgery is available which can be performed in late teens. Nevertheless, with ongoing developments, hopefully this philosophy will one day no longer be necessary.

I feel very privileged to have been one of the first generation to undergo surgery to correct MR. I also feel proud to consider that members of my treatment team were substantially involved with the Sri Lankan Cleft Lip and Palate research project and care programme.

In chapter seven I commented on the fact that, unless a cleft is a facet of a life-limiting condition or syndrome, it is not a life-threatening condition within the developed world. However, in impoverished nations there can be a risk of severe complications in the case of clefts, especially if repair surgery is not available or cannot be afforded. This would be due to potential problems respecting feeding if affected babies are unable to maintain sufficient nutrition or food ingestion. When considering the plight of babies/children and adults in such nations of the world as Sri Lanka who are affected by clefts, it is quite thought-provoking to realise how easy it is to take the NHS for granted, where babies born with medical conditions such as clefts can automatically receive basic treatment without families having to worry about such issues as availability and cost.

One extremely significant development respecting cleft care during my lifetime was the foundation of the Cleft Lip and Palate Association (CLAPA) in 1979.

CLAPA supports individuals who are affected by cleft lips and/or palates, their parents and families from the time of a baby's diagnosis through to completion of treatment in early adulthood.

A significant number of geographically regional groups known as 'CLAPA communities' exist across the United Kingdom. Such groups comprise patients, parents and families, health professionals and volunteers, researchers and additional personnel who are dedicated to helping CLAPA to take positive and active roles in shaping the future of cleft care and making the world better place for all who are affected by clefts in the UK.

Specific support offered by CLAPA includes many spheres; examples including the following.

*Support for parents on receiving a diagnosis of a cleft, virtually always through antenatal scans nowadays.

*one-to-one emotional support from trained volunteers, including parents of children born with clefts.

*Specialist feeding services including the provision of feeding equipment.

*Events and meetings led by health professionals which concentrate on various subjects related to cleft care.

*Liaison between health professionals, volunteers, patients and families.

*Enabling patients to meet and encourage each other by sharing common experiences and treatment.

*Visiting schools where pupils with clefts attend in order to raise awareness of the condition among peers.

*Social events such as Christmas parties and summer camps in order to bring children and young people with clefts together to share experiences and realise that they are not isolated.

*Provision of opportunities for individuals, parents and families to express opinions, needs and concerns.

*Adult Voice Council, forums, etc.

In recent generations, there has been recognition and acceptance of the fact that adults who were born with clefts can require and benefit from support which was unavailable when they were children/adolescents. However, through CLAPA's formation and development over the years, such support is now accessible.

CLAPA is a godsend for parents whose babies are affected by a cleft. I know just how much my parents and myself would have appreciated CLAPA during my infancy and childhood.

Following a CLAPA event some years ago, I was invited to join a family at lunchtime. The father had been born with a cleft lip and palate and one of his children had inherited a cleft. The father had been affected by MR but, being older than myself, corrective surgery was unavailable in his adolescence/early adulthood.

The father was a university lecturer, but he spent much of his schooling in the low academic streams because many of his teachers assumed that he had low intelligence due to his speech and appearance.

The father stated the amazing differences between his own experiences of hospital treatment and those of his child, and said how much he wished that CLAPA had existed when he was born and growing up, for the sake of both his parents and himself.

Although ignorant and prejudiced mindsets respecting disabilities will probably never be completely eradicated, attitudes have fortunately vastly improved in recent generations regarding the presumed connections between physical medical conditions and learning/cognitive delays or disabilities.

Delays or disabilities respecting mental development are not symptoms of clefts alone, so, unless babies who are born with clefts are affected by an additional disability or the cleft is a facet of a more serious condition or syndrome, problems which are related to learning or cognitive development will never be an issue for children who are born with clefts.

The final welcome development which I have observed during my life has been the much stronger rapport between medical professionals, parents and children themselves if they are of an age to be able to ask their own questions and express their own opinions and concerns.

I have referred to such issues in previous relevant chapters, especially chapter three, in which I recorded differences between my first and second operations. Obviously such improvements have continued in ratio in successive generations.

As shared in chapter four, GOSH itself is gradually being completely rebuilt, much redevelopment having already been completed. Many original hospital buildings have been or are in the process of being demolished.

On attending a GOSH Children's Charity event in 2019, I felt rather lost, since the hospital was almost unrecognisable compared with my previous visit some years earlier! I felt totally amazed and overwhelmed by the transformation, with its ever-increasing contemporary approach to children's care and treatment.

As in all areas of life, it is only when looking backwards that one realises how time progresses!

On my first ever appointment at GOSH in autumn 1960, the hospital probably looked impressive and 'state of the art' in its generation, with the nurses wearing their traditional smart uniforms. However, nowadays, with the ongoing redevelopment of the hospital, nurses and indeed all staff sporting contemporary uniforms, photographs of GOSH as I knew it in my childhood look distinctly primitive, although I will always feel privileged to have been a 'Child of Great Ormond Street'.

I felt that it was appropriate to include a Medical Addendum in order to acknowledge both my own experiences in comparison with the past and future generations regarding all aspects of the care of sick children, physically, mentally and emotionally.

BIBLIOGRAPHY AND SOURCES OF REFERENCE

NIV Bible 2011, from which the vast majority of Scriptural texts are quoted.

(The) Chapel of St. Christopher: Great Ormond Street Hospital for Children NHS Trust, by Raymond J. Lunnon, Curator, The Museum & Archive Service, GOSH NHS trust in consultation with the chaplaincy.

(Hospital chapel brochure copyright 2002 re-printed 2005) Bibliography re text- St. Christopher's Chapel-Peter Larkworthy,

Great Ormond Street and the story of medicine, J. Kosky and R. J. Lunnon, Granta editions 1991

Other material from Museum and Archives Service Record Photography: Department of Medical Illustration, UCL, ICH and

GOSH for children, NHS trust "Spiritual Care for all"

GOSH "Pioneer" Journal Summer 2020 edition (acknowledgement for both text and photography) Children First and Always: Derrik and Gillian Mercer Macdonald publishing (GB) First published 1986

(The) Remarkable story of Great Ormond Street Hospital: Kevin Telfer pub Simon & Schuster UK Ltd. 2008

(The) Golden Book of Peter Pan, pub. George Newnes Ltd. copyright 1965

Management of Cleft Lip and Palate: Alex Habel, Debbie Sell, Michael Mars-

BMJ pp361-365 pub. 2001) acknowledging both text and photographs on p364)

(The) Boy David-Marjorie Jackson pub. BBC 1985

London Hidden Interiors: Philip Davies Atlantic Publishing 2012

New Town Naughty Boy-Richard Blackshire Copyright 2015 Richard Blackshire, pub by Amazon

Lightning Source UK Ltd. Milton Keynes UK A More Excellent Way: Be in Health

Spiritual Roots of Disease; Pathways to Wholeness by Dr Henry W. Wright, Pleasant Valley Publications (USA) First published 1999

A More Excellent Way: Be in Health by Dr Henry W. Wright, Whitaker House publishing (USA) First published in 1999

Natural Solutions to the Menopause: Marilyn Glenville (Rodale publishing 2011-USA)

On the Spectrum: Autism, Faith, and the Gifts of Neurodiversity by Daniel Bowman Jnr., Copyright 2021 by Daniel Bowman Jnr. published by Brazos Press, a division of Baker publishing group www.brazospress.com, printed in USA

The Shack: Wm Paul Young in collaboration with Wayne Jacobson and Brad Cummings, Copyright William P. Young 2007 Windblown Media, first published Hodder & Stoughton 2008; A Hachette Livre UK company

Through the eyes of hope: Lacey Buchanan (with Bethany Jett) Copyright: Lacey Buchanan 2017, Charisma House Books

Wonder: R J Palacio. Alfred A. Knopf/Random House publishing 2012

You are Special: by Max Lucado., pub. Candle Books copyright M. Lucado 1997

CONTACTS AND USEFUL SOURCES OF INFORMATION

NATIONAL AUTISTIC SOCIETY
391–393 City Road, LONDON EC1V 1NG Tel: 020 7833 2299
Fax: 0207 833 9666
Email: nas@nas.org.uk Website: autism.org.uk
BEREAVEMENT PERSONNEL CHRISTIAN FELLOWSHIP
(BPCF)
Website: www.bpcf-online.org.uk
CHANGING FACES
PO Box 76751 LONDON WC1A 9QR Tel: 0345 450 0275
Email: info@changingfaces.org.uk Website: www.changingfaces.org.uk
CLEFT LIP AND PALATE ASSOCIATION (CLAPA)
The Green House, 244–254 Cambridge Heath Road, LONDON E2 9DA
Tel: 020 7833 4883 Website: www.clapa.com
GREAT ORMOND STREET HOSPITAL CHILDREN'S CHARITY
(GOSHCC)
40 Bernard Street, LONDON WC1N 1LE Tel: 020 3841 3841
Email: supporter.care@gosh.org Website: www.gosh.org
AGLOW INTERNATIONAL
PO Box 122, SOUTH SHIELDS NE33 4WU Tel: 0191 456 4232
Email: nationaloffficebrittain@aglow.org.uk Website: www.aglow.org.uk
Living Hope Ministries
Email: lhm@livinghopeministries.uk
Website: www.livinghopeministries.uk
OPEN DOORS
PO Box 6, WITNEY, OXON. 0X29 6WG
Tel: 01993 460015
Email: inspire@opendoorsuk.org
Website: www.opendoorsuk.org
GUILD OF CHURCH MUSICIANS (GCM)
3 Sewards End, WICKFORD, Essex. SS12 9PB Tel: 01268 733817
Email: gcm@rjandrews.me.uk Website: churchmusicians.org
ROYAL SCHOOL OF CHURCH MUSIC (RSCM)
19 The Close, SALISBURY, Wilts. SP1 2EB Tel: (initial/general enquiries)
01722 424848
Fax: 01722 424849
Email: enquiries@rscm.com Website: www.rscm.org.uk

THE AUTHOR

Katy Christopher was born in Hertfordshire and, with the exception of college years, lived in the village of Abbots Langley until she moved to Lancing, West Sussex following her marriage to Hugh.

Although Katy and Hugh do not have their own children, they gain much pride and joy from their official and honorary nieces and nephews, goddaughters and sons and their families.

Katy and Hugh are members at Lancing Tabernacle Evangelical Free Church (known as Lancing Tab).